BUILDING FREEDOM

BUILDING FREEDOM

A Construction Pro's Path to Financial Independence

David Gerstel

LATITUDE 67

Publisher's Cataloging-in-Publication data
Gerstel, David, author.
Building freedom : a construction pro's path to financial independence / David Gerstel.
Includes bibliographical references and index. | CA: Latitude 67, 2021.
LCCN: 2021917831 | ISBN: 978-0-9826709-2-7
LCSH Construction industry. | Contractors' operations. | Small business--Finance. | Finance, Personal. | Success in business. | BISAC BUSINESS & ECONOMICS / Industries / Construction | BUSINESS & ECONOMICS / Personal Finance / General
LCC HD9715.A2 G47 2021 | DDC 624/.068--dc23

Copyright © 2021 by David Gerstel, Author

Developmental Editor: Jackie Parente
Copy Editing: P&M Editorial Services
Proofreading and Indexing: Toni Briegel
Cover and Interior Design: Deb Tremper at Six Penny Graphics

All rights reserved. No part of this book may be scanned, reproduced, or transmitted in any way or form without prior permission from David Gerstel

Printed and Bound in the United States of America
First Trade Paperback Edition December 2021

An important note to the reader: This book is intended to stimulate your own thinking about your purpose, possibilities, and principles. But you are, of course, responsible for developing your own path to financial independence and for seeking legal, financial, and other counsel as you deem necessary. The author and all other persons associated with the publishing of *Building Freedom* shall have no liability to any person or entity with respect to any loss or damage caused or alleged to be caused directly or indirectly by information, concepts, practices, strategies, or description of materials, methods, or equipment described herein.

For additional information please contact us at DavidGerstel.com

A Note from the Author

I hope you enjoy *Building Freedom* and that it helps you down your own path to financial independence. If so, you may find it worthwhile to read and hear more of what I have to say by visiting my website, *davidgerstel.com*.

At *davidgerstel.com* you will find reviews of my other books:
- *Nail Your Numbers: A Path to Skilled Construction Estimating and Bidding* became a construction industry bestseller shortly after it was published. It comprehensively lays out the bidding and estimating systems crucial to the success of any construction company.
- *Crafting the Considerate House* is a nonfiction narrative about the design and construction of a home that is attractive, affordable, and environmentally considerate. Written as a story, *Crafting the Considerate House* entertains even as it provides useful ideas on design, cost control, and sensible green building.
- *Running a Successful Construction Company* has long been called "a bible" of the construction industry. The most recent edition is now two decades old and does not cover recent advances in digital devices and software. But it continues to get five star reviews from readers because of its clear discussion of the essentials of construction company management.

At *davidgerstel.c*om you will also find a selection of my articles as well as links to podcasts where I have appeared as a guest.

A contact form is provided on the website for readers who want to get in touch with me. I greatly enjoy hearing from readers, so if you feel like it drop me an email.

All best, David Gerstel

Contents

Prologue: Freedom, Oliver, and Max 1

I. **Preparing Yourself** 13
   - Your Right Stuff 15
   - Lean and Frugal 27
   - The Employee Centered Company 35
   - Thought Remodeling 45
   - Keeping Purpose in Mind 53

II. **Building a Profit Engine** 63
   - The What and the Why of Profit 65
   - Constructing Profit Opportunities 75
   - Numbers 89
   - Protecting Your Profit 107

III. **Building Financial Intelligence** 121
   - Managing Cash 123
   - Investment Literacy I: Principles 129
   - Investment Literacy II: Practices 139
   - Deploying Capital 149
   - Friction, Debt, Max, and Taxes 161

IV. Anchoring Financial Freedom 171
- Investing in Your Construction Company 173
- Investing in Real Estate I: Possibilities 185
- Investing in Real Estate II: Execution 197
- Investing in the World Economy 211

Epilogue: Beyond Financial Freedom 225

Tools 231
Essential Resources 239
Glossary 243
Appreciations and Acknowledgements 251
Index 253

Prologue:
Freedom, Oliver, and Max

Let me clarify one thing right here at the beginning of this book. Building financial freedom, as I understand it, is not about getting really rich. It is not about having far more wealth than you will ever need. Financial freedom is simply about getting past the point where you will have to work to pay your bills.

After you get to that stage of your life, you may continue to work. In fact, if you have the drive, discipline, and decision-making capability required to reach financial freedom, you likely won't be happy not working. You are the kind of person who needs responsibility, who needs to be on the move. You need to release your creative energy. But once you are financially free, working for income is not a necessity but a choice.

Achieving financial freedom requires more than hanging out a shingle and going into business for yourself. When you start your own business, you may then be free of "the man." You are done with the bosses you've grown tired of serving.

Having your own business is not the same thing as being financially free. You can be your own boss and be far from free. That's a lesson learned by many skilled trades people who decided to set up as independent professionals working with clients rather than in someone else's company. They have found themselves manacled to the enterprises they created, working exhausting hours and feeling harassed by subcontractors, customers, and crew. I know a builder whose company generates $25 million a year doing high-end residential remodeling. He feels trapped in his never-ending responsibilities. "This could be a pretty good gig if it were not for clients, trade partners, and employees," he sighs.

Creation of a strong construction company may be your necessary first step toward financial freedom. It can be the source of the means necessary to get to financial independence and beyond. That's why we will discuss key features of a strong construction company in several coming chapters.

To move beyond running your own business to financial freedom you must go further. You must acquire investments that will produce the income you need to live on. The investments will reliably do that through strong and weak economies. They will produce the income with only minimal monitoring and management on your part.

Because they require little maintenance, they are termed "passive investments." Ben Graham, author of *The Intelligent Investor* – a seminal work about investing that advocates a low maintenance approach to financial management – said that he hoped every day to do something creative, something generous, and something foolish (i.e., fun). A substantial but still relatively small and simple portfolio of passive investments can enable all that.

As construction pros, we are fortunate to be in a position to acquire the investments necessary for freedom. We know how to create a product – shelter and infrastructure for homes, businesses, and public entities – for which society has an ongoing need. In other words, we have potential customers, a lot of them.

We also have access to education in the skills necessary to win those customers and build our strong – i.e., financially sound, though not necessarily large – businesses. The education is available at modest cost in books, courses, and conferences. It can even be extended at no cost with careful listening to the best podcasts.

Yes, we are in an industry where it can be difficult to make money and frighteningly easy to lose it. But the difficulties can be overcome. Financial success is within reach. As we will discuss in an upcoming chapter, "Building a Profit Engine," even a micro- or small-size construction company can be developed to the point where it will generate considerable earnings. It can produce ample income for its employees and owner to live on. At the same time, it can deliver the surplus cash needed for those investments that enable a life of creativity, generosity, and fun, and is free of financial pressures. We can build structures for our communities and at the same time build freedom for ourselves.

The road to financial freedom is open to aspiring construction pros. Some construction pros travel the road successfully. Others veer into a ditch. Consider the experiences of Max and Oliver.

Max and Oliver met when they were in their mid-twenties. Max was working as a carpenter. With the country in deep recession, he had a difficult time staying employed. Repeatedly, he would find a job, then be laid off and told, "Sorry, but we just don't have anything else going right now. Stay in touch, buddy." Max would drive around town, stopping at every construction site he found and asking for work until someone hired him.

One morning, he came upon a crew forming a foundation on a steep hillside. Oliver was running the crew for his father-in-law, a veteran builder who had survived the Great Depression by working as a carpenter on the construction of the Hoover Dam and then made his way into home building. Oliver sized up Max – his near mirror image at six foot plus, lean and muscular, with a full beard – talked to him for five minutes, and said, "You can start now."

Max built two houses with Oliver. Then Oliver's father-in-law hit a slow period and ran out of work for Max. He recommended Max to a woman who lived across the street from the second house. "The young man's a hard worker, and he won't bullshit you," he told her. She hired him to build a deck. After Max completed it, she referred him to friends who needed work done on their places. He built more decks, rebuilt decayed walls, renovated bathrooms, hung and finished drywall in a basement room.

Each job led to others as satisfied customers recommended Max around their social network. He never stopped to wonder why. But in later years he would realize that he gave his customers the same thing he wanted from the men and women he hired onto his crews. He got to work on time, worked steadily, and was passionate about doing things right. If he was intimidatingly straightforward at times, customers preferred that to being lied to or manipulated, just as Max would later prefer employees who were candid with him.

Max had no conscious idea of how to go about what is now called "building a brand." He had never imagined going into business for himself. But after a time working with clients, it dawned on him that he had somehow created a business with a good reputation. He liked the independence. He liked deciding for himself what to do and when to do it. After that first deck, Max never again worked in someone else's company.

Occasionally, Max talked with Oliver, who had also gone into business for himself. Oliver was building spec houses in a booming town north of the city where he and Max had worked together. Oliver always sounded confident. Business was "smokin'," he said. He was making a name for himself. "It feels good to be the up-and-coming young man about town."

Though they were not nearly the size of Oliver's new homes, Max's own projects were growing in scope. He moved up from repairs and minor improvements to steadily larger remodel projects. He gutted and rebuilt kitchens and offices, constructed additions, added second stories to one-story structures.

Max liked the work. Six days a week, he was out of bed at dawn, on the move, and busy till dinnertime. Occasionally he felt overwhelmed. He had to create relationships with subcontractors, set up accounts with suppliers, and assemble his first crew.

Finding good people and coordinating them during a project was a new challenge. As a carpenter he had first learned to fit things together. When he began managing projects involving multiple trades, he'd learned to fit processes together. Now he was learning to fit people together. He was evolving from a tradesman into a manager and executive.

He liked his new roles and the steep learning curve. At times, it felt daunting. Often, he would abruptly awaken at three a.m., sweating with anxiety, imagining that he had overlooked a major item of work when putting together his estimate and bid for a job.

He had bad dreams, too, about mistakes at a jobsite. And now and then he would make one. He had never been trained in flashing and waterproofing. The first pair of French doors he installed leaked. So did a skylight. Drywall fasteners popped on one job because the studs he had installed were too green. Late one afternoon, after he and his crew had completed the final details on an especially satisfying renovation project, Max loaded his tools into his truck. Distracted by his exuberance, he backed his truck straight into a new Corvette parked at the curb across the street from his project.

Max forced himself to own up to the mistakes and fix them. He did groan inwardly when customers called him back to a job to fix a defect. "I hate callbacks," Oliver had told him. For a time, Max agreed. But gradually he realized callbacks were great marketing opportunities. Clients had heard so many stories about builders who did not stand behind their work. They were relieved, even grateful, when Max promptly took care of problems. His responsiveness deepened clients' trust in him and prompted them to enthusiastically refer him to their friends.

Max confessed to the Corvette owners about the damage he had done to their new car. They waved off his offer to have his insurance company pay for the damage. They said they were glad to meet an honest builder. Might Max be available, they asked, to remodel their kitchen?

Getting a handle on business management systems was even tougher for Max than fitting material, processes, and people together at his jobsites. Unlike Oliver, who had earned a business degree before going to work for his father-in-law, Max's education had been in the liberal arts and science. Business was new and confusing territory for him. Accounting, with its specialized language and maze of reports and statements, especially frustrated him.

Years later, looking back, he wondered how he had survived with so little knowledge. "I had never even heard the term 'business systems.' I did not know what marketing was, much less that marketing and sales were not the same thing. I had no training in how to do either one. I had never seen a construction estimate. I had never hired anyone, much less highly skilled people for several crews and a team of subcontractors. I did not know accounting was a management tool. I thought it was just for keeping track of your tax obligations. I guess I just kept putting one foot in front of the other. I'd find a book or a veteran builder who would explain things to me. Slowly, I got the hang of business, and good jobs kept coming my way."

Max enjoyed a surge of happiness every time he got a call from another person wanting to entrust him with their project. The requests for his services made him feel valued in his community. He was beginning to make good money, too.

From his mentors, Max gradually learned to climb the compensation ladder. At first, he charged only for labor, including his own, and for material and subcontractors at cost. But he came to understand that he must charge also for the out-of-pocket costs of running his company and for his work as company manager. Max even moved to charging for preconstruction work – not only for design but for his detailed estimates and his proposals for cost management on projects.

Crucially, he learned to incorporate a charge beyond the charges for his costs and expenses and the value of his own work. In other words, he learned to charge an actual profit.

That last step was hard for Max. He had been educated to view "profit" as equivalent to "greed." But he got over it. He did remain uneasy about maxing out profit at his clients' expense. He wanted to offer them a good deal. But he also came to believe in the necessity of profit for reasons we will discuss in coming chapters.

Oliver, too, was expanding his business. He sold his first spec house and plowed the profits into additional lots. He built and sold more houses and bought more lots. Within a few years, Oliver had eight new houses under construction. Meanwhile, he constructed a new home for his family on a twenty-acre spread overlooking a river. He invited Max up to see it.

His father-in-law, Oliver told Max, was telling him to slow down. "That's that Great Depression mentality. The Old Man is stuck in it," Oliver said. "The Depression made him scared for life. He's got that rule, never start a new house until the previous one is sold. That keeps him small-time. He misses a lot of opportunity." Oliver said he had no intention of slowing the expansion of his homebuilding business.

Max was impressed by Oliver's confidence and capability and felt envious of his home. He hoped that he would someday be able to have such a place. Even so, he let his own business grow slowly, building each project as well as he could and creating a growing network of satisfied clients who recommended him to other clients.

Instinctively, he disagreed with Oliver's criticism of his father-in-law. Max could not see that passing up opportunity was somehow failure so long as you were steadily notching up successes. He knew that the Old

Man had done that, had worked his way from laboring on the Hoover Dam to ownership of sizable real estate holdings.

"Why," Max puzzled, "is it failure to pass up some opportunities if you are making good on others?" Though he could not yet have articulated it, Max was beginning to formulate what would become one of his cardinal business principles: It is not the mistakes of omission that really cost you. It is the mistakes of commission.

If you passed up a big, juicy project because you felt you weren't quite ready to handle it, you might feel regrets. But you'd suffer no harm. On the other hand, taking on that project, when in fact you were not ready for it, could bury you in losses.

Max analogized the situation to tennis. You might regret passing up an opportunity to maybe hit a winner. But the omission would not ruin you for the match. You had to be patient, waiting for good opportunities to hit winners, and meanwhile avoid unforced errors, that is, ruinous acts of commission.

One sunny summer morning, Max was laying out wall sills and plates for a new addition. He heard his name called. Max turned to see Oliver in his pickup. He took off his tool bags and invited Oliver to pull over for a chat.

Oliver got out of his truck, offering a wide smile and a strong handshake. He spoke at first with his usual easy confidence. Soon he switched to talking about problems. Payments on the bank loans for the eight houses he had under construction were coming due. But the houses were not selling. A new recession had set in. It was accompanied by steeply rising interest rates on mortgages. That discouraged people from shopping for homes.

Max could see that Oliver was seriously worried, but he did not know what to say. Oliver was operating in a territory too far from his own world of remodel and renovation projects. The two young men shook hands and wished each other good luck. Oliver got back in his truck and drove off.

Though his business was still very compact, just one crew and a few trade partners, Max had been steadily saving money. He suggested to his wife that they use their savings to buy a home. They found a cottage they liked and made an offer. It was accepted. Max and his wife took on a mortgage and bought the cottage.

Oliver came to see their new place. He admired the wide plank flooring and the setting with its views of the hills. But about his own situation, he spoke angrily. "The banks," he said. "They want to be your pal when you are doing well. When you really need them, they squeeze you for all they can get."

Oliver did not stop by again. From a mutual friend, Max learned that Oliver's business had collapsed. Mortgage rates had continued climbing. They went to 12 percent on their way to 17 percent. At those rates, there were no buyers for the eight houses Oliver had built.

Hoping to stave off the bank while he sought customers, Oliver mortgaged his new home for the cash needed to make his construction loan payments. But interest rates did not drop. The houses did not sell. The bank took them, foreclosing on one after the other. Then the bank took Oliver's home.

After learning about his friend's hard times, Max occasionally tried to find him. Over the years, Max would occasionally ask other builders if they knew where Oliver had landed. He asked about him in the town where Oliver had built those eight houses. But no one had any idea where he was.

Max was puzzled. He felt sure that Oliver had somehow bounced back. Where, he wondered, and how? He often thought of Oliver but, as the years passed, gave up trying to locate him. Meanwhile, Max went forward, learning, doing good work, enjoying customer references, and storing up money. He saw that financial freedom was a real possibility, something he could achieve well before conventional retirement age. He began to invest.

He felt lucky. "I am a blessed guy," he would often tell friends.

For a time, he would encourage other people to make their way into construction. He thought being a construction pro was a great way of life for people who liked autonomy, being creative, and making money. Then he began to see that many people who went into the construction business did not have such good fortune as he had. More than a few crashed as badly as Oliver had. Others seemed to be just limping along after many years in business.

"Why?" Max wondered.

I wonder myself. Just at the time I was writing this book, I learned of an experienced builder who operates a small company in a prosperous metro area. He had lost $250,000 on a project. Over the years, I have heard worse stories. Way too many of them.

What brings on such misfortune? Is it just the result of eagerly reaching for what looks like a great opportunity and then getting in over your head? That is sometimes the case. Thinking they are taking a big step forward, builders get involved with projects they are not equipped to estimate, much less build. Or, hungry for work, they put themselves at the mercy of an unscrupulous client or incompetent designer and a contract weighted against them.

There are, as well, broader reasons for their misfortune. Melanie Hodgdon writes of the "generous craftsman syndrome." Hodgdon is a financial consultant. She chooses to work with construction pros because she admires their pride in craft and their honesty.

She is troubled by their outcomes. "The very characteristics which make them good neighbors too often leave them with little in the way of pay to show for their efforts." For decades they do work that makes them proud, but they underprice it. They take care of their employees. They take care of their customers. But they fail to tend to their own needs. Finally, they are "worn out" and facing a future of financial worries.

Another financial advisor sees an opposite problem: arrogance. Construction pros are susceptible to it when they hit a hot streak in a hot economy. They begin to fancy themselves masters of the universe. They open a trophy office with a big shiny table in a big conference room and tool about town in a luxury SUV or truck. They borrow money to turbocharge the growth of their companies. When hard times strike, they don't have the financial reserves to get through them.

Tim Faller is a former remodeler who now hosts a podcast. He cautions young builders who have come up during construction booms against getting the big head. Do not, he tells them, mistake results enjoyed during the good times to be a sign of your exceptional prowess.

He's warning against what the ancient Greeks called "hubris." That's the thought error that leads you to think you are above the rules and can fly like an eagle when you should be working your fields like a plow horse. Max wondered if hubris had been Oliver's problem. Max himself happened to admire plow horses more than eagles. He counted himself lucky for that.

There are choices to be made. To my way of thinking, choosing a steady, plow horse-like road to financial freedom is a good choice. It's a good choice even if you imagine that once you have the investments that enable freedom you might want to take some of your assets and use them to finance an experiment at flying like an eagle.

With the great bulk of your investments held back to ensure your freedom, your attempt to fly high will be far less stressful. You will have a safety net. You will know that if your experiment fails, you won't be wiped out along with it. You will land in the net instead of crashing into financial desperation.

In my own career as a construction pro, guided by mentors I discovered along the way, I was able to steadily travel the road to financial freedom. I decided to write this book about the road as I understand it. I am sure it is not the only road. But it is one I know well. I believe it is one that is accessible to many construction pros.

I have tried to keep the book short and focused. I don't want it packed with roadside attractions that might distract readers from the road itself. To that end, I have included only crucial and illustrative how-to material. There's plenty more of it – procedures for marketing, checklists for bidding and estimating, explanations of accounting, and methods for evaluating investments – in the resources, including my own books, listed at the end of this book.

Building Freedom is about choices and strategies. It is about possibilities, purpose, and principles. Let's get to them.

PART ONE:
Preparing Yourself

- Your Right Stuff
- Lean and Frugal
- The Employee Centered Company
- Thought Remodeling
- Keeping Purpose in Mind

Your Right Stuff

During my decades in construction, I have followed the careers of many men and women who have done well in both residential and commercial work. They are deeply engaged with their work, whether it's remodeling or building new structures. They make good money. They achieve financial freedom, sometimes early in life. I have wondered what distinguishes them from the many others I have known who struggle, just muddle through, or outright fail. What's their right stuff? What, are the ingredients of their success?

I wish I had exact answers. I don't. I have encountered other writers who promise their readers a "secret sauce." I don't have one. All I have is considered impressions, mine and those of others who ask similar questions.

In my world, the people with the right stuff generally came up through the trades. There are exceptions. I know one builder who started out about as far as you can get from dirt, lumber, and nail guns. He began his career as a financial analyst, moved to banking, specialized in packaging loans for home builders, monitored their project sites, and became so fascinated that he jumped into residential construction. Over the course of a decade, he moved from struggling to renovate small cottages to competently building large custom homes.

But typically, the successful construction pros I am acquainted with started out working with tools and material in the heat, the cold, the mud, and the dust. They became skilled at the hands-on, minds-engaged, bodies-on-the-move tasks of on-site, minute-by-minute, day-by-day construction. That experience advantages them when they take on estimating and production management. Both tasks require capability at envisioning how structures will be put together. Construction pros with deep trade experience know how that's done. They can see the work happening out in the future with their mind's eye.

You may have come up through the trades. You may have come over from banking (though probably not). But regardless of where you started, if you are on the road to financial freedom, you have the character of the entrepreneur.

You are a person inclined to create not only products, but an enterprise. You have the stuff celebrated by great American enterprisers going all the way back to Benjamin Franklin (who started out in the trades himself). You are certainly not reckless, but you are bold when you see a good opportunity. You want to step up and take charge. You have that can-do attitude. You do not hesitate to tell that first possible customer, "Sure, I can handle that for you" – even if you need to do some homework before you actually can.

You do handle that first job, and you handle the jobs that follow, even as you are rocked by challenges and work crazy hours. You battle through confusion. You get exhausted. You feel discouragement. But you fight it off. If you hit hard stuff, you tend to go toward it, not away from it. As John Bogle – the founder of Vanguard, which now manages investments for 30 million customers – emphasizes, you don't have quit in you; you *never* quit.

As you build your enterprise, you temper determination with humility. You realize you have much to learn. You seek teachers and find them in books and at construction associations. You are willing to learn from anybody. Perhaps you remind yourself (as I often must remind myself), "Idiots can't learn from wise men, but wise men learn from anyone, so shut up and listen."

You pursue luck. You understand that if you stay on the move, good things are likely to happen. You realize that the more you network with fellow builders and your larger community, the better your chances of running into mentors and opportunity.

Even as you enable luck, you go hard at your day's work. You aim to produce durable structures. Your framing is plumb, level, and square. Finish work is crisp, joints are tight. About insulation, air sealing, and water and moisture management, you are fanatic. No gaps or leaks allowed.

Your trade partners share your insistence on quality. Your plumber's copper joints are clean. No solder dribbles down their supply lines. Level five drywall finish is wiped so tight that sunlight cascading down a thirty-foot-long wall does not cast the slightest shadow.

The day may come when you put down your tools to devote yourself to running your company. Even then you do not become so focused on marketing, sales volume, and profit percentages that you let the quality of your construction slide. You understand that durable and good-looking work delivers long-term financial success and personal satisfaction.

Building failures are humiliating, undermine your reputation, and cost money. Good work makes you proud and wins the support of your clients. It enables you to hang onto your earnings and – rather than spend them on warranty work and lawsuits – invest them to secure your financial independence.

When you first went into business for yourself, you may not have understood that you were entering a whole new world. You may not have realized how much leadership, managerial, and financial competence you would need to acquire. As Dan Kolbert, a veteran builder, wrote in *The Journal of Light Construction*, our "typical progression" is to work in the trades, start doing side jobs, gather a crew, move up to bigger and more complex jobs, then discover we "are doing half a million dollars a year" but don't know where the money is coming from or where it is going.

It is at that point – if you have the entrepreneurial drive encouraged by Franklin and Bogle – that you hit the books. There is hard study ahead. You realize you have to learn about business systems and build them.

You must create a marketing program. You need it even if satisfied customers steadily refer work to you. You need it to refresh and encourage their referrals. You need it so that potential new customers will readily find you and be encouraged to get in touch.

You must construct bidding and estimating procedures with the awareness that bidding and estimating are *not the same thing*. Bidding is an executive, a leadership, function. When you decide to bid or not bid for a project, you are determining whether it will take your company in the right direction. You are considering whether it is the kind of work you want to be doing. You are evaluating whether it will take you into relationships with people you want to be involved with, or not. You are calculating the charges you must include in the bid to sustain your company during the project and earn a profit as well.

You understand that estimating, in contrast, is grind-it-out management work – arguably the most critical work you do along the road to financial independence. If they are to move you forward, bids must be accompanied by accurate projections of your costs of construction in the field. When they are not, the financial setbacks can be brutal. When the estimates are reliable, job after job can deliver financial reward along with the creative satisfaction of building.

So you roll up your shirtsleeves and build a system for producing those accurate estimates. You learn how to use an electronic spreadsheet. You embed in it a comprehensive list of all the items of work that occur in the kinds of projects you do. You use it to make certain you are picking up every detail in a job and accurately tallying their costs.

You are determined, also, *not* to be one of those builders who has only a vague idea of how many hours a crew will need to do the work required by a project. You are going to be the exception. You are going to be the guy who assembles the data necessary for dead-on estimating of your labor costs – typically the most elusive costs in a project.

You build a file of labor productivity records like the sample record provided in the "Tools" section at the back of this book. With each job you do, you add to your records. Relying on the records from completed projects, you accurately forecast labor hours on upcoming projects.

Along with creating labor records you establish procedures, like those described in upcoming chapters, for obtaining reliable subcontractor and supplier quotes. Your goal is to build an estimating system that will enable you to come within a couple of percentage points of your projected financial outcomes on project after project. Others have done it! So why not you? You keep improving your estimating system till you reach your goal.

Builders who like building sturdy structures get satisfaction from creating a strong estimating system. When estimating, you are imagining the fitting together of all the parts of a project. You are constructing it in your head. Personally, I think estimating rocks. Good estimators are skilled craftspeople.

Another critical system can, however, feel much more abstract and less approachable. That is accounting. At the outset of their careers, many construction pros think that accounting is merely about keeping track of income and expenses in order to fill in the blanks on tax returns.

That is one of the purposes of accounting. Construction pros with the right stuff understand that the bigger purpose is to enable financial management of a company. A good accounting system enables you to track and understand the movement of money through your business.

To comprehend accounting, you can think of a construction company as a system of pipes through which money flows. You must be able to see in detail where the money is flowing from. You must be able to see where it is going.

Accounting enables that vision. It divides the flow of money into progressively smaller pipes according to its origins and destinations. Did the money arrive as payment for design work? For other preconstruction work? Or did it arrive as payment for completed construction work? And was that work at the Harris jobsite or at the Wangs' place?

Did it flow out for work at the Wangs'? Or for work at the Harris place? Did it flow to a trade partner, an employee, or a building supplier? Or is it going for the expenses, from paperclips to computers, of running your company?

Good accounting software will answer those and other questions in response to your feeding it numbers from a keyboard. It will display them in organized reports. It will give you a clear view of where your money is coming from and where it is going. It will do all that for surprisingly little cost. We will take a more detailed look at accounting in "Numbers," coming up in Part II.

Even if you have the entrepreneurial determination to create the systems discussed so far, you may recoil from the next one: the construction contract.

Maybe "contract" spells "lawyers" to you. Maybe your friend Joe, a masonry contractor, got fleeced by a lawyer representing a worker with a phony injury claim, so you hate lawyers. Or maybe you are like the builder who believed his clients so adored him that he did not need a contract. "They love me," he said. He believed he was one of those superior people who could do business on just a handshake. At least he believed that till one of his clients took him for $100,000, due to his lack of attention to the legal niceties. Is there need to say more?

With marketing and sales, bidding and estimating, accounting, and a contract in place, you have the primary business systems you need back at your office. Of course, you must also systematize production at your jobsites. You need procedures for ordering material. You must establish efficient and consistent patterns of communication with crew and clients.

You need Gantt charts – simple bar charts that display the sequence in which trade work is done and the length of time that work should take. Gantt charts are indispensable tools for scheduling your subs and determining whether your project is on schedule. You can easily create them with pencil and paper or with low-cost computer applications.

You also need people policies. You must establish guidelines governing the behavior of yourself and your team when attending to company business. You need procedures for evaluating, hiring, positioning, and, when necessary, terminating your crew members and office people. You want the right people on your team. You want them playing in the position that is right for them, for your company, and for yourself.

Say you are employing an unusually skilled carpenter who happens to also be self-centered. You may assign that person to demanding carpentry work like building staircases with elaborate balustrades. You do not make them a lead carpenter. A person concerned primarily about him- or herself is not the right person to put in charge of other people. (I know from having made that mistake myself.)

Systems and systematic procedures are a must in construction. You'll find extensive how-to guidance on creating systems and procedures, including Gantt charts, in the books listed in "Resources."

It may be true for many types of businesses, as experts often insist, that the main cause of failure is lack of capital. Restaurants and retail shops, for example, need to invest heavily in inventory and equipment before opening their doors. They need money on hand to pay their bills while they gradually acquire customers. If they run out of money before they can ramp up their earnings, they are finished.

Certainly, as we will be discussing, construction businesses need capital in reserve to get through hard times and for other reasons. You can, however, start a construction business with little more than a reliable used truck, tools, a phone, and a computer on a worktable in a corner of your home. As your company develops, you can gradually strengthen its systems, again for relatively little cost. Construction companies, except for those operating heavy equipment, are not capital intensive.

From what I have seen, construction companies don't collapse primarily because of lack of capital. Their problem is inadequate development of management systems coupled with overreaching. They do not have the procedures in place that will enable them to handle those bigger jobs or larger volumes of work that tempt them. They take on too much business and then struggle to take care of that business.

Once you have created systems, how do you make sure you are using them effectively? One simple gauge: Ask yourself, have I created and am I using checklists – just a simple list of items that must be accomplished and checked off – for all the basic tasks my business must regularly accomplish?

Do you have a checklist for qualifying a project for a bid? Do you have one like that displayed in the "Resources" section at the back of this book for the site inspections that are essential for creating accurate estimates? Do you have checklists for your marketing work, for sales calls, for your weekly and monthly accounting tasks, for hiring and firing, for all of the business management that your company must attend to?

Are you religiously using those checklists?

If your answer is yes, good. Is your answer no? Then, if you are serious about traveling the road to financial freedom, it's time to construct your checklists and begin using them relentlessly.

I am not the only one believes that. In his highly respected book *Traction*, the business educator Gino Wickman reports that countless studies attest to the value of checklists. Their use, he emphasizes, results in significant improvement in performance of all operations from quality control to project management.

Does all this demand for systematization put you off? I went over it with a skilled tradesman who was considering going into business for himself. His response: "You are scaring me."

Are you like him? When confronted with the demand to get organized do you shake in your boots? Are you inclined to run the other direction? Or do you insist to yourself, "I am going to wrestle that stuff to the ground." If you are scared by the demands, perhaps you should continue working for other people. If not, then you may have the right stuff to build a successful construction company.

Beyond procedures and checklists there are softer aspects of entrepreneurship. There is the matter of leadership. A big deal is made of it in the business world. Numerous books delve into it. Consultants offer coaching in it. Colleges offer courses about it.

I find the whole discussion of leadership unnecessarily complex and overwrought. Yes, a construction pro with the right stuff needed for long-term success must have leadership abilities. But as far as I can tell leadership boils down to a willingness to initiate enterprise, take charge, and adjust direction as necessary.

For the construction pro, leadership can be summed up in a few sentences: Ally with people who want to work hard, produce quality work and value integrity over cleverness. Treat them all – employees, customers, trade partners – with respect and consideration. Expect the same in return. Make sure to practice and demonstrate integrity yourself.

As you explore leadership and entrepreneurship, you will likely encounter exhortations to take risk. You may be urged to take on projects that, by any reasonable calibration, are too big a step beyond anything you have already done.

When it comes to investing, you will hear even more insistent demands. Certain financial gurus urge that you must just go for it. Fail to do so and they will condemn you for timidity.

Discount such go-for-broke counsel. Yes, some folks are excessively averse to risk. I have a friend who becomes terrified, ducking her head and wrapping her arms around herself, at the mere mention of the word "risk." If you are afflicted with severe risk aversion, you will have to find a way to overcome it in order to travel the road to financial independence.

However, if you are a construction pro, especially if you have started your own company, risk taking is likely not a big problem for you. You have chosen to work in one of the riskiest of all enterprises (writing books is the only one I know of that is riskier ☺). Risk does not scare you off.

Benjamin Graham's take on risk is useful for construction pros who want to get to the point in their lives that work is a choice, not an economic necessity. Graham's book, *The Intelligent Investor*, is built around the concept of taking risk productively by maintaining a "margin of safety." That is the most important advice about business I have ever encountered. It urges carefully sizing up, calculating, and managing risk, not merely jumping into it.

Knowledgeable risk management must accompany risk taking. You don't just charge into a project several times the size of any you have handled before. You don't act on hot tips from someone who tells you about a "can't lose" investment. Both in the management of your company and in investing, you learn to assess risk and consider the possible outcomes. In coming chapters, we will return to "margin of safety" and look at tools for evaluating risk. As you will see, it's like stealing bases in baseball. You hone your understanding of when to stay and when to go.

With system building, consistent leadership, and risk management, construction pros put themselves in a good position to make it down the freedom road. That's not to say the journey will be easy. The going-out-of-business rate for construction companies is sobering. While the stats vary, it appears that about three-quarters are gone within five years. Of the survivors, three-quarters are gone by the end of the next five years. Bottom line: Out of every 100 construction business start-ups, about half a dozen are still in existence ten years later.

To be among the survivors, you probably need some luck, both that granted by fate or by a higher power, and that which you will create for yourself. You will need to land in the right place at the right time.

The good news: To a considerable extent, you already have. If you have come across this book, it is likely that one way or the other, you landed in the United States. You are in a country that offers tax breaks in exchange for enterprise, legal practices that offer protection against rip-off artists, and solid business education available at low cost.

With construction, you have chosen work that can enable you to accumulate the capital needed for the investments. You are in a line of work that may, cruel irony, benefit from the disasters that befall other people.

Floods or fires wipe out neighborhoods or even whole towns. They create work for construction pros. Even a worldwide pandemic may play out in your favor. The onslaught of COVID-19 benefited many builders, especially residential remodelers. Their customers were stuck working from home. They noticed all kinds of projects that needed doing around the house. They called their favorite construction pros.

The continuation of our good luck is not guaranteed. Industry observers like Barry LaPatner, a Manhattan construction attorney and author of *Broken Buildings, Busted Budgets*, lament the persistent existence of smaller construction companies run by independent pros. They call for the "industrialization" of construction. They would like to see it consolidated into a few megacorporations pumping out buildings the way a few automotive companies produce all our vehicles.

So far, efforts at such consolidation have not succeeded. Yes, production builders have taken over a large portion of the new home market. But the production builders typically work with trade partners to build their developments. Smaller companies can do well as their trade partners. One, in Nashville, Tennessee, has built a thriving business handling punch lists and final cleanup for production builders. All told, there is still space in every sizable town and city for many independent construction pros.

Those willing to make the steady effort to build systems, exercise leadership, and practice risk management have something else going for them. They enjoy an advantage in the marketplace because so many of their competitors will not make the effort. Those guys are like a builder I met long ago. A book was recommended to him that would have taught him how to build the business systems he badly needed. He blew it off. Too expensive at twenty-five bucks, he said. Anyhow, he did not really need it. He could just eyeball a job and figure what it would cost to build it. And that office stuff, the wife took care of that.

Last I heard, his wife got tired of taking care of business for him. She filed for divorce. His company collapsed. He was working as a salesperson in a window store.

In other words, construction pros who willingly do the work to cultivate their right stuff benefit from the incompetence of those who will not. The incompetents will disappear. Often, they leave behind disappointed clients. Next time out, those folks will pay good money for construction pros who do take care of business. And some of those pros will discover principles and practices, such as those discussed in our next chapters, that enable financial freedom.

Lean and Frugal

In the 1990s, two college professors, Tom Stanley and Bill Danko, set out to answer a question: In the United States, who are the wealthy people? By "wealthy" they did not mean super rich. They meant people who were financially free, who could stop working and live off cash flow from their assets. Stanley and Danko wanted to know: Where do these people live? What are their consumption habits? What are their values?

Drawing on the databases of the Internal Revenue Service, Stanley and Danko did huge amounts of research. They organized their findings into a book titled *The Millionaire Next Door*. A finding that is of particular interest to us here: The great majority of the millionaires in the U.S are self-made. They own small businesses. A good many of them are construction pros, what I like to think of as "pickup truck millionaires."

Danko and Stanley called the financially free folk "millionaires next door" (MNDs I call them for short) because of their lifestyle choices. They are far from miserly. They tend to live well and do not deny themselves comfort and pleasures. But they are thrifty and are not attracted to luxury. Their houses are of modest size. Mostly they settled into pleasant but distinctly middle-class areas and remained there. They buy used cars, take care of them, and keep them for a long time. They are far more likely to wear a Timex than a Rolex.

The MNDs do not think much of people who use their money for signifying. They don't deck themselves out with fancy stuff to show other people how important they are. The MNDs suspect that below all the flash may be a depleted bank account. Texan MNDs dismiss the signifiers with four words: "Big hat. No cattle."

When Stanley and Danko first began to study their millionaires next door they did not expect to find such modest levels of consumption. They associated high consumption with wealth. They assumed the wealthy were heavy-duty consumers.

During their research for their book, the two professors were contracted by a financial services firm to do a study of people with a minimum net worth of $10 million. To suitably host their interviewees, the professors rented a penthouse. They hired caterers to lay on a spread of caviar and expensive wine. Their first guest arrived. He was wearing a well-worn suit. Missing the cue, one of the professors asked if he might pour the gentleman a glass of the "superb 1970 Bordeaux." The guest stared at him. "I drink two kinds of beer," he said. "Budweiser and free." He emphasized "free."

The story of the Bordeaux and the Budweiser appears in a chapter of Stanley and Danko's book, titled "Frugal Frugal Frugal." That could just as well be the title of the book. It is their passion for frugality that explains the MNDs. It is the source of their preference for modest homes, Timex watches, and free beer. It is also the wellspring of their financial freedom. Their money goes into investments, not consumption of things they do not need.

You will remember Max from this book's prologue. At the time his friend Oliver's homebuilding business collapsed, Max was just beginning to see the possibility of the freedom realized by Danko and Stanley's "millionaires next door." He had not yet begun to build cash flowing investments – the investments which would provide a stream of income and free him from the need to work for financial reasons. But as he took the first steps with his business, he was instinctively practicing the frugality characteristic of MNDS and building a lean operation.

Max set up an office in an unused corner of his home with furniture and supplies purchased at yard sales or built from door blanks and lumber left over from his projects. He bought his first truck, a twenty-five-year-old Dodge pickup, for $150. He did not upgrade until he could buy a newer truck for cash. Then he settled on a used Ford, in great shape and with low mileage, that he figured would give him many years of service.

Max shared the MNDs preference for durable but moderately priced clothing. He heard two veteran builders debate the best way to dress for a meeting with an upscale client. One argued for an expensive dress shirt and a sports jacket because "you want them to think you are one of them." The other said, "No, go meet them in jeans and work boots, clean but not polished. Then the client sizes you up as a guy who earns his pay." Max went for the clean boots option.

Max, as is surely the case for many other pickup truck millionaires, was also disposed to the frugal use of time. Oliver and Oliver's father-in-law had taught him that in construction the meter is always ticking. It's ticking fast. Time is money.

Time and motion efficiency, Max had learned, is vital to financial success. You do not go looking for a crowbar to lift a wall frame off the floor. You drive the claw of your hammer into the top plate and yank the wall up. Always, you consolidate movement. You do not measure, cut, and fasten, and then go through the cycle over and over again. You make all your measurements, all your cuts, and then install all the pieces you have prepared. Movement is thereby reduced. Time is saved. Money is made along with structures.

"Those little savings, they add up," Max said to the builder friends he gathered with to talk about business once a month. "Get rid of fifty or a hundred dollars' worth of inefficiency every workday. That can add up to $25,000 a year." He did not then mention, as he would later in his career when he understood investing, that the $25,000, put into a retirement accounts, could readily grow to $450,000 in a few decades.

Charles Schwarz might not like to think of himself as a construction pro. He's a woodworker based in Kentucky. But woodworkers and construction pros do essentially the same thing. They set up for projects, acquire equipment, bring in materials, cut it, shape it, fasten it together, and deliver something useful and beautiful to their customers.

Charles is not only a construction pro. He is the co-owner of Lost Arts Press, a publisher of books about furniture making. He blogs from its website. His blogs offer good thinking for construction pros of all stripes, especially around exercising frugality to create a lean business.

In a blog titled "Cutting the Cord" – freeing yourself of the need to "work for the man" as Charles puts it – he tells us about a few of his frugality measures. Each year he reviews his internet provider's rates to make sure he is using the lowest cost service that meets his needs. When renewing subscriptions to his professional journals, he asks for the introductory rate and gets it. Annually, he checks with his insurers to make certain he is enjoying all applicable discounts.

Charles avoids interest payments. He pays none because he does not borrow money. He and his wife, Lucy, decided against debt early in their marriage when they were twenty-three years old.

Costs, Charles says, are like fingernails. They grow to unsightly proportions if left unclipped. He says he could add ten thousand more clippings to the list of frugalities mentioned in his blog. Certainly, he could. New opportunities to pare down even a lean construction company are forever appearing in our shifting economic landscape.

Our consumption-driven society often contemptuously equates frugality with stinginess. The practice of frugality does require judgment calls. You can go over the line and become penny wise and pound foolish. Effective frugality requires staying on the right side of the line. Descent into stinginess can result in waste. Frugality avoids waste. It is about *the careful cost-effective use of resources*. It's about running lean, not starving yourself or your business into weakness.

Charles advises that when you buy a tool you should buy a well-made and durable tool, though it will likely be more expensive than other options. I agree. When you are building a lean company, you purchase only what you need. But then you purchase quality so that you will not soon have to purchase again. Personally, when I buy a computer I buy the most expensive brand on the market. I have learned that product long outlasts the cheaper brands and is supported by superior service. It saves me money and time over the long run. Plus, it's more elegantly designed.

Frugality can be a foundation of personal freedom. It enables generosity. It is about caring for the earth, because each time we consume, we damage. That is why, when I make something for my home or rental houses, I make it out of salvaged material if possible. I save money. I reduce environmental damage. I get satisfaction from repurposing older material of good quality.

Frugality has enabled me to become financially free. It has put me in a position to help others. I don't always get it right. One of too many possible examples: From thoughtless frugality – also egotism, for I was excessively proud that my company was in such demand that we were always busy without my investing a dollar in marketing – I never purchased jobsite signs. They would have cost money for manufacture, installation, removal, and storage.

By never spending on jobsite signs, I did save a few bucks. But at a cost. A couple of times my steadfast crew suffered through replacing foundations under houses with shallow crawl spaces. A small investment in signs would likely have brought in more pleasant work to fill our schedule. The crew would not have had to labor on hands and knees digging trenches and forming stem walls.

Frugality becomes foolish miserliness when it is misapplied in the management of a construction company. Running lean with elimination of unneeded cost and wasted motion is frugality. Squeezing employees, chiseling trade partners, and cutting corners on quality is mere miserliness. It is counterproductive.

Stinginess with employees contributes to turnover, which can be brutally expensive. Squeeze your trade partners, and they will move on and spread the word: "Stay away from this guy." Cut corners and you will experience building failure, which impairs reputation and imposes severe dollar costs. Assign a low-wage laborer rather than a skilled craftsperson to install flashings, and you'll be back at the jobsite repairing the decay and damage caused by leaks. Hire a cheap and marginally skilled plumber, and you might get a call from a customer on Christmas Eve when a failed supply line dumps water through the ceiling above their bed in the middle of the night. That's what happened to me before I had fully learned my lesson.

Unfortunately, there is a fad afoot in the construction world encouraging miserly practices that can do long-term damage to your financial possibilities. Its adherents declare that making profit should be your highest priority. The profit-comes-first approach instructs you to take a profit off the top of every payment you receive during a project – before paying any of your bills for labor and material and subs at the project, or for the costs of running your company during the project – and to set that profit aside in a hands-off account.

With the profit safely stashed away, you must, according to the profit-comes-first theories, then complete the job and run your company with whatever dollars are left over. Some construction pros who encounter such ideas are enthralled. They seem to think they have found the pathway to riches. I doubt it. Taking profit first can encourage cutting corners. It can leave you without enough money to produce good work and manage your company effectively. In the long run, that will cost you, not enrich you.

Neither costs for production at the work site nor the expenses for running your company should be treated as leftovers. Instead, labor and material costs should be controlled and honed so that high-quality work is produced with ever-improving efficiency and effectiveness. The off-site costs of company management should be similarly controlled.

The control must be achieved without cutting corners and with focus on doing good work.

As you build a stronger and stronger reputation for that good work, you can, to the extent your market allows, steadily increase your profit charges. In short, you are not taking profit off the top. You are taking profit when you have earned it. You will have earned it by building an efficient, lean, and trusted company that can charge prices that include substantial profit – something well beyond what you charge to cover all your costs including pay for your own work.

In my experience, if there is a single factor that most supports profitability, it is generosity toward the people you work with. Charles Schwarz seems to have come to a similar conclusion. Intently frugal though he is, he writes with pride of paying top dollar to the designers and editors who help him produce his Lost Art Press books. Though he works and lives in Kentucky, they get "New York rates."

Schwarz has apparently discovered for himself the lesson I first learned from reading an interview in a business journal. The interview was with Mr. L.L. Bean, the founder of the famous clothing company. Mr. Bean taught me that you get a generous return on your investment when you when you pay generously; that if you pay 20 percent above market rates, you will get a 50 percent better employee.

At the same time, pay itself is not enough to reap that return. It must be part and parcel of a broader generosity. That's the subject of our next chapter.

The Employee Centered Company

All of us in the construction business ask ourselves, even if not quite consciously, "What kind of company do I want to create? What values and practices do I want to build into it?" Our answers are visible in the orderliness (or slovenliness) and safety (or dangerousness) of our jobsites. They are apparent in the quality of our installed foundations, mechanical and electrical installations, and finish work. They can be heard and seen in the morale and capability of our crews and in our own behavior. Together, the answers indicate the character of a company as surely as a person's values and practices reveal their character.

During his two decades in construction, my friend Sam Mills has worked as a carpenter, as a project lead on residential work, and as a supervisor of large commercial remodels for a series of construction companies. Often we talk shop. Sam emphasizes that the companies he has worked for get very different results and that, in his opinion, those differing results arise primarily from their owners' differing degree of willingness to look at their behavior. "When you have a problem, especially one that comes up repeatedly," Sam believes, "you should first look at yourself to ensure that your actions are not the root cause of the problem."

Sam has found the habit of "looking within" in short supply. Too many of the builders he has known thought that they could solve their problems from outside themselves. "Not getting the respect you deserve? Buy a bigger truck. Not as successful a contractor as you want to be? Buy elaborate accounting and estimating software. Hire a hot shot carpenter away from a competitor."

"Their egos are too big," Sam reflects. "They always think they are just an expenditure away from 'rocketing into the stratosphere of success'" (as one of his bosses actually put it). They see problems and solutions as outside of themselves rather than as originating within themselves or stemming from the character of the company they have created and led.

After a decade working on the East Coast, Sam moved back to Colorado to be closer to his family and went in search of a new job. He was not looking for a higher salary or a more prestigious position. He was hoping to find a company that shared his values. Sam had his hopes up. During a phone interview with a company he thought looked promising, the owner had hit the right notes, emphasizing energy-efficient construction, steady management, and concern for workers.

When Sam arrived at the company, he was given a tour through its headquarters. The company occupied a large building featuring post and beam detailing and an expansive warehouse and shop. To Sam, that looked like a lot of overhead for what was a midsize residential remodeler.

His skepticism increased when he was taken to the company's jobsites by the company's production manager. He saw that all the workers were young and learned that none had more than a few years' experience. The production manager complained that they constantly made mistakes.

Sam learned that the PM was himself a self-taught and marginally capable carpenter. He saw that the PM and his inexperienced crew were trying to build from skimpily detailed drawings produced by the company's in-house designers. Sam was disappointed. The company was loaded with material assets. But it had made only an anemic investment in people. That was not the sort of company he had hoped to find. Sam understands that a construction company does not derive its main strength from its shell – its office, shop, warehouse, trucks, or computer systems. It's not a creature with an exoskeleton. Its strength is internal, coming from the motivation and capability of its workers in the field and in the office.

Strong construction companies are what I call "employee centered." A construction company can thrive with remarkably little in the way of material assets. It cannot thrive with a stingy investment in people.

What does an employee centered company look like? How does it behave?

It treats its employees and trade partners with respect. To begin with, they are greeted, always, by name. That may seem like a small matter. It is not. As Dale Carnegie emphasized in his book *How to Win Friends and Influence People,* to each of us our name is the most important of all words.

Some years ago, the founder of a much-admired construction company with an experienced and loyal crew sold his company to an ambitious younger man. The founder thought he had the right guy to carry forward his legacy. He did not. The new owner soon burdened the company with heavy debt and excessively risky projects. Meanwhile, as one senior project manager angrily commented, "he did not bother to learn the names of new people" as they were hired into the company.

In 2007, a severe recession hit. Perhaps the company would have gotten through it had the new owner been able to get the support of his veteran employees. He did not get it. His disrespect for his employees had alienated them. The company went bust.

Some builders have honed their disrespect to a lacerating edge. A lead carpenter described her experience with a new boss. "She would walk on the job and say, 'Am I running a fucking daycare center?'"

When a problem came up at the project, the owner told the carpenter, "Come in on the weekend and fix it on your own time." The carpenter felt like she had been "punched in the gut." To herself she thought, "Really, it's me against you. We are not in this together?"

Construction contractors in general undervalue the importance of respect. *The Journal of Light Construction* asked a group of workers and a group of construction company owners to rank ten factors in order of importance to worker morale. Workers listed respect first. They put pay midway down the list. Owners had their workers' priorities exactly backward. The owners put pay at the top of the list and respect halfway down.

Top-notch construction companies treat their employees not as underlings but as co-workers. They let the co-workers know, "We are all in this together." One company notable for its employee centered practices – along with its steady growth and profitability for close to half a century – underscores that message on its website. There it features a photo of every one of its eighty employees from apprentice carpenters to the CEO. Under each photo is the employee's name.

This company also had a tough time during the severe recession of 2007. About a year into it, I asked the owner how the company was doing. He said, "We are resilient. We're doing everything we can to get through this, and we will." Notice the use of "we." The owner has co-workers, not just hired hands. They express their high regard for him often. They are with him. He and his employees did get through the recession. They have thrived during the recovery.

The employee centered company manifests respect in many ways: By asking employees "What could we be doing better?" and actually acting on the feedback. By steadily expressing appreciation for work well done. And by refraining from micromanaging and instead giving as much autonomy to workers as is practicable. Autonomy is high on that list of what workers said they wanted from their company. It comes just after respect.

In the employee centered company, workers are included in the decision making that affects their lives. I once got an abrupt reminder of the importance of that. My company used a four-day workweek. The crews were at their jobsites Monday through Thursday. Then they were off work until Monday morning. The crews loved their four-day workweek and for years had organized their lives around our Monday-through-Thursday work schedule.

One afternoon, I announced to them that I was changing the schedule so that they would be working Tuesdays through Fridays. They just stared at me or nodded or mumbled something and went back to work. I climbed into my truck and headed off to my next stop. Later in the day, my senior project lead phoned me. "Everyone is furious about the schedule change," he told me. "They are all talking about quitting."

I apologized and reversed my decision. But it took me awhile to appreciate the magnitude of my mistake. The crew had long counted on having Fridays off. With no warning, I had taken Fridays away from them and disrupted their lives. I had treated them as pawns I could move around on my chessboard at will. Fortunately, the crew accepted my apology. No one quit. The experience nudged me toward a new gesture of respect toward the crew. Whenever I considered a project for a bid, I asked crew members whether they would like to build it before I contracted with the owner for preconstruction services.

At that point in the development of our company, our projects often lasted the better part of a year or even more. When we took on a project, we were determining how a crew would be spending a major part of their time and energy for a long while. I realized they should have a say in the determination. No one on the crew ever said no to a project I wanted to go after. They also never told me they appreciated being asked. But I am pretty sure that my asking strengthened the sense of "we are in this together." I remember their smiles when I gave them a set of plans and asked them to let me know whether we should go after the job. "Yeah, looks good to me," they would report back.

Running an employee centered company really comes down to abiding by that golden rule recommended by the most famous construction pro of all time. Yes, that carpenter from Galilee named Jesus. He told us, "Do unto others as you would have them do unto you."

If you or I were an employee, how would we want others to do unto us? We would want to be addressed by our name. We would want to be treated as a co-worker and not as a pawn. We would want to be shown respect and given autonomy rather than being micromanaged.

As part and parcel of respect, we would want good pay that recognizes our worth. Pay may not be their first priority. But that does not, of course, mean that employees don't care about pay.

Pay and respect are joined at the hip. Good pay is a gesture of respect. It says, "You are valued." Poor pay is demeaning. It says to a worker, "You are not worth much to me."

Employee centered companies aim to provide workers with good wages and benefits. The owner of that company that survived the 2007 recession and thrived afterward takes pride in offering the highest level of compensation available in his area.

Good pay can be provided in a variety of ways in addition to wages and benefits. One is a safe workplace. The owner of a construction company in Maine is ardently frugal. He uses resources with great care. Neither he nor his company has any debt. When his company improves its systems, it pays for them with cash that has been put away in a savings account. The owner is always on the lookout for equipment that will protect workers from injury. When equipment that enhances safety comes on the market, the company purchases it. That surely emphasizes to the employees that they are valued.

In employee centered companies, you will see owners prioritizing employees' pay over their own during hard times. If pay must be cut across the company, they take the first and biggest cut. One owner cut his own pay by a third during a major recession, and only then asked his highest paid employees to take a 10 percent cut. Lower-paid people were not asked to take any cut at all. When work began to pick up, the owner restored his pay last.

Employee centered companies often share profit with their employees. That declares emphatically, "We are a team, we are co-workers. We sow together. We reap together." That frugal company in Maine provides its employees not only with safety equipment but with a share of its profits amounting to as much as 14 percent of their wages. The company provides its employees with education about how to invest their profit share in order to eventually secure financial freedom for themselves.

Employee centered companies have made a striking modification of that old business adage: "The customer is always right; the customer comes first." *Small Giants*, a book about a wide range of highly successful companies, vividly describes the extraordinary service they provide to their clients. But "what really sets the small giants apart," the author observes, "is their belief that the customer comes second." Their employees come first.

I agree with the revision. I think it is a smart adjustment. I think it is smart because of the benefits to an owner of running an employee first company. Those benefits include the financial results necessary for building freedom. The company takes care of the employees. The employees take care of the clients. The clients become repeat customers and bring good new clients to the company.

In my experience one of the most powerful ways of putting employees first is use of the four-day workweek (with nine-and-a-half-hour workdays). It is a gesture of appreciation and respect. It acknowledges that workers have lives beyond the company. It recognizes their need for freedom, the very thing owners (at least those who are reading this book!) seek for themselves.

In other books, I have pointed out all the ways in which the four-day week provides benefits to a company along with workers. Among them: The owner is free to entirely concentrate on management and leadership tasks during the extra off day. There's no interruption by job site concerns. Clients often welcome the extra day of quiet at their properties. Production is more efficient because set-up, break down, cleanup, and similar daily costs are incurred 20 percent less often, i.e. four rather than five days a week. Altogether, the benefits of the four-day week greatly outweigh any mild inconveniences.

Because so few construction companies offer the four-day workweek, the company that does enjoys increased loyalty. Workers don't want to give up their four-day workweek. They tend to stick around. Along with profit sharing and other expressions of respect, the four-day week can greatly reduce turnover – with its heavy costs for hiring, training, and maybe firing and hiring again after a hiring mistake.

Low turnover signals that you are building an employee centered company. Another sign, as *Small Giants* reports, is employees developing "a deep sense of belonging, of ownership." Even outsiders will notice it. An architect says of a construction company both she and I admire, "They are a band of brothers. They have each other's backs." In my company, I felt we were getting to that sense of belonging and ownership when the crew began to say, "our company."

Sometimes acting from the belief that employees (and equally your trade partners) come first does impose short-term cost. At a remodel, my hardwood flooring installer had done his usual superb job. The client, however, was upset that the new flooring did not exactly match her existing oak flooring, battered and erratically stained though it was. They told me to have the installer tear out his work and redo it to match the old flooring. If I did not, they threatened, I would never get a reference from them.

Out of the question, I told my client. I was not about to tell my flooring guy to destroy his beautiful work. They made good on their promise and never did refer my company to another client (though during a phone conversation ten years later they did tell me that they loved their kitchen and that the flooring was great).

My flooring installer stuck with me and gave priority to my jobs. He produced great work for many customers. Their friends saw it and called our company for their projects.

Is it not likely that well-respected and fairly compensated employees, and trade partners, too, will be motivated to make your company a success? I think so. Not everyone, of course. But yes for the kinds of people I want as co-workers in my business and that you probably want in yours.

That's why, in the context of the construction business, I sometimes think of the golden rule – treat others as you would like them to treat you – as the "*very* golden rule." Abiding by it delivers gold to you, as the owner of a construction company, as well as to your workers and trade partners. To put it a little differently than I did a few pages ago: You do for them. They do for your clients. The clients return the generosity. They recommend you around town, helping you to build a profitable operation and acquire the capital necessary to secure financial freedom.

In short, running your company so that it is employee centered is just enlightened self-interest.

Let's be clear here: Running an employee centered company does not mean that you bend over backwards to always be a nice guy. You are a demanding guy. If you run an employee centered company, you expect a lot back. You set the bar high. You give respect. You expect respect in return. You require workers to treat one another with respect. You require them to do top-notch work for your customers and to treat the customers with the consideration they receive themselves.

You expect your people to work hard, both physically and mentally, looking always to improve efficiency. You expect company tools to be handled with care. If you see an apprentice carpenter lay a circular saw on its guard, you greet him by his name and explain to him how to set down a saw without damaging it. You expect him to not make the mistake again.

Your message is clear: "We do things right here. If you don't, you are gone."

If you run an employee centered company, you run a tight ship. When you see leakage – waste of time and motion, waste of material, negligence with tools – you put a stop to it. Otherwise, the company will fail in a major responsibility to employees. That is to be profitable. If it is not, it will go under, and the employees will lose their jobs.

If you do try to run an employee centered company, you can't expect to get things right all the time. It's kind of like parenting. In many of life's tests, the highest score you can go for is 100 percent. But in parenting the highest possible score is 70 percent. No one has ever gotten it.

Ditto for running a construction company. We have to make countless judgment calls. We won't get every one of them right. If we do find ourselves coming up short repeatedly, Sam Mills's advice can stand us in good stead. Don't look for an off-the-shelf solution. Look inward first to find the source of the problems. Look at your values and behavior. Look at the thinking they arise from.

Thought Remodeling

"Bob," as I will call him here, has been in business for twenty-five years. He designs as well as builds most of his projects. They are skillfully crafted, durable, and beautiful. Bob takes great care of his clients, but not of himself. He woefully underprices his work. For the bathroom or kitchen remodels that are his specialty, he charges half the going rate for other established builders in his market.

Bob's underpricing results from what psychologists term "thinking errors," self-defeating ideas that we play back to ourselves over and over. Bob's makes the errors that are called "mind reading" and "catastrophizing." Bob believes he knows how his clients view him. He has convinced himself that they see him as a "handyman," not worthy of higher pay. Bob aims to get nine out of ten jobs that he bids. That's three times the rate generally considered acceptable by savvy builders. Whenever he loses a bid, he begins playing out apprehensions of doom: It's over. I'm done for. I will never get another job.

The concept of thinking errors originated with psychologists looking for a way patients who suffered from depression or anxiety could help themselves.

They came up with a straightforward procedure for correcting thinking errors: Identify a destructive thought pattern. When you find yourself slipping into that error, quench it. Will yourself to replace the destructive thought with a more reasonable thought (not an excessively optimistic thought, just a reasonable one). At some point your brain will hardly be capable of thinking the old dysfunctional thought. It will, according to brain scientists I have spoken with, literally disappear from your neurological pathways.

Psychologists call the brain training "cognitive behavioral therapy (CBT)." I think of it as "thought remodeling." It is useful for more than dealing with the thinking errors that damage our mental health. It can be employed to correct the misconceptions that impair management of our construction businesses.

Take Bob's error. It's one that many construction pros make. They too have convinced themselves they will never get another job if they raise their prices to the level charged by established builders in their area. Some have silenced such thoughts. They have gradually raised their prices to the level enjoyed by their competitors and discovered that they continue to win clients and contract for projects.

They have banished their thinking error from their brain. They no longer believe they have to charge bargain basement prices to get work. They have replaced that belief with thoughts like "Our prices are what you have to charge if you want to do good work, properly take care of your customers, and stay in business." If the old fear of not getting work creeps back into their brain, they kick it out and remind themselves, "I sell value, not price."

Numerous thinking errors and misconceptions plague our construction industry. Each of us invents a few for ourselves. Here I will focus on several that I consider to be among the most destructive – and that, unfortunately, are encouraged by folks who, though they have never run a successful construction business, have set themselves up as "strategic advisors" in our industry.

Certain of these advisors will tell you, "Concentrate on doing what you are good at and let us experts look after your accounting." In other words, just work on your projects. Swing your hammer. We'll take care of the numbers.

No! If you are a construction pro who has gone into business for yourself – especially if you want to arrive at financial independence – you cannot remain oblivious to accounting. That's like trying to build a house without a tape measure. *You must know your numbers.*

You may seek advice on setting up and using whatever accounting software you choose to keep tabs on your company's financial performance. But you must understand what numbers must be fed to the software. You must understand what output is needed and why it is needed. You must be able to comprehend the information and make use of it to measure your company's financial performance so that you can manage it effectively.

To get to that point, you likely will need, for a while, to handle the accounting chores, the bookkeeping, yourself. Just as with the construction trades, the best way, maybe the only sure way, to get a sure grip on accounting, is to get into the trenches and do the work. You can't just dump it on someone else (like your spouse), turn your back on it, and expect to succeed as a construction pro.

Particularly hazardous thinking errors occur around accounting for "overhead." As mentioned earlier, overhead expenses are those incurred for running your company, as opposed to your "direct costs" of production – namely costs for trade partners, labor, and material at your jobsites. In accounting lingo, "overhead" is termed "SGA," which stands for "selling, general, and administrative expenses." That is a good summary of the expenses that make up overhead.

Importantly, just as your direct costs include any labor you personally do at your jobsites, your overhead includes the value of the work you do managing and leading your company. In other words, if your overhead accounting is in order, it will include two categories of expenses: out-of-pocket expenses for everything from paper clips and computers to salaries for staff; and into-your-pocket expense, namely the so-called "owner's pay" that you take for running your company.

The purpose of accounting for overhead is to monitor and manage it. For as we have emphasized in "Lean and Frugal," overhead control is crucial to building financial freedom. To control it you must account for it. You must know just where it is occurring in your operation.

Even construction pros who have long been in business for themselves fail to track their overhead. They do so because they are oblivious to it. Many pros, especially those with small operations, proudly declare "I don't have any overhead." Really? No office space, computer or software? No phone, office supplies, furniture, insurance, truck, or tools? None of your valuable time expended on sales calls, on estimating and bidding, on reading your construction journals to keep up with new developments? No costs for subscriptions to those journals?

In fact, those are all SGA expenses. In *Nail Your Numbers*, my book about bidding and estimating, I list seventy-two discrete categories of overhead expense. Soon after they go into business for themselves, when they are basically a one-person operation, any construction pro is likely to have half of those expenses. After building just a small company with a few employees and trade partners, they will incur nearly all of the seventy-two overhead expenses.

Dismayingly, overhead obliviousness and the failure to monitor and then manage overhead is sometimes encouraged by certain of the aforementioned "advisors." I was astonished to hear one tell clients to focus on four numbers: sales, estimating, the costs of construction (i.e., job costs) and profit margins. The production manager for a company, instructed the advisor, should focus on sales and estimating. The owner should concentrate on construction costs and profit margins.

No one was given the task of keeping track of overhead. You see the problem? Not even the owner was advised to keep an eye *on the costs of running their own company.*

Such obliviousness can severely impair the financial performance of your company. It can undermine your prospects for achieving financial freedom. The *more* you spend for overhead, either in the form of out-of-pocket costs or owner's pay, the less of your income remains as profit. The less *you* spend on overhead, the more income you retain as profit.

The more profit you retain, the more cash you will have available for the investments that support financial freedom. Without properly accounting for overhead, you won't know just where you are incurring it. You will be far less likely to be able to manage it, control it, and make space for that additional profit.

As Max advanced in his career, he became aware that getting beyond the point he had to work to pay his bills was a possibility. He saw that vigilant overhead accounting was critical to realizing the possibility. Every dollar spent unnecessarily for overhead was a dollar diverted from his investment program. Thorough accounting enabled him to keep a close watch on overhead.

Max had looked for books that would help him understand investing. He had come across one that delivered a crucial lesson: Saved dollars, if invested, can grow with stunning force due to the power of compounding.

We will go into compounding in detail in later chapters. Here it is enough to report what Max saw as he came to understand the phenomenon. He calculated that by carving out an office in an unused corner of his home rather than renting office space he could save $800 a month, $9,600 a year. If he invested just that one year of savings it could, at historically average rates, compound to $434,000 over the course of his career. If he invested the savings every year of the next forty or so years he expected to work, well, the possibilities amazed him.

As he worked at the job of running his company, Max did not repeatedly run such numbers through his head. He simply reminded himself that the total income from his projects was like water that filled a barrel. Because he was committed to producing high-quality work and paying his crew top dollar, the bottom two thirds of the barrel would have to flow out for the cost of construction. Of the top third, some portion had to go for computers, phones, business software, tools, and other inescapable SGA expenses.

Max kept in mind that the less he spent on such "out-of-pocket" overhead and the more he restrained that other overhead expense, his owner's pay, the better. More would be left at the top of the barrel for profit that he could put into long-term investments. In other words, overhead control would provide him with the financial resources he needed get beyond the point he had to work for monetary reasons.

Max tracked his overhead expenses in detail with his accounting software and pared them back vigilantly. He held out-of-pocket overhead expenses to a percentage less than a third of what was typical for small construction companies. Max chose, also, to go the millionaire-next-door route. He poured out just enough in pay to himself to maintain a lifestyle that was comfortable and healthy for himself and his family.

His strategies worked. They resulted in ample profits. He shared them with employees because he felt that was the right thing to do and an act of enlightened self-interest. It proved to be. His crews stuck with him. They produced "bulletproof" work. Max hung on to the profits. They did not go back out the door for callbacks, building failures, or litigation.

Max invested his share of the profits prudently. The value of his investments compounded. Max moved steadily toward his goal.

A misconception as severe as obliviousness to overhead, and that likewise is broadcast by certain strategic advisors, is this: "If you are not growing, you are dying." By that, the advisors mean that if you are not growing your volume of sales you are somehow failing at business. "Grow or die," they insist.

Their axiom needs revision. It should be changed to "Grow sustainably." In other words, grow only when you have the capability to produce increased volume profitably. Too many construction pros who have lunged after sales growth and increased volume for its own sake have, as a result, failed in business. They have had to start over after taking tremendous losses or going through bankruptcy.

Let me post a warning here: I have noticed that the "grow or die" idea is pushed by certain industry consultants who benefit from their clients' growth without sharing in the attendant risks. Their income is tied to their clients' revenue, not the clients' profit. So the higher the revenue, the greater the consultants' income. They can reap a reward by implanting the "grow or die" thinking error in their clients' brains. They don't suffer nearly as much as a client if a client overreaches and goes bankrupt. Be leery of those guys.

Let's give Paul Eldrenkamp the last word on the subject of growth. Paul is the founder of Byggmeister, an unusually stable, long-lived, and well-run design/build firm in Massachusetts. In one of his superb articles for the *Journal of Light Construction*, Paul declared, "When times are good it is harder *not* to grow than to grow, so we all look like marketing geniuses. When the next recession hits, all this talk of growth will disappear and the hot topic will be survival. The companies left standing, I predict, will be those that have resisted growth for growth's sake."

Just as we must remodel our thinking to overcome obliviousness to overhead and the "grow or die" delusion, we need to shed a misconception about our balance sheets. A balance sheet, as you know if you have your accounting stuff together, is a financial report. It lists all your assets, such as the value of a pickup truck. It lists all your liabilities, such as the amount you owe on the truck. With all the assets added up, and all the liabilities subtracted, the balance sheet gives a figure for the financial net worth of your company, say $211,997.

Here's the misconception: Thinking that a balance sheet with a heftier positive bottom line is a good thing in and of itself. After all, more net worth is better than less, right? Being richer is better than being poorer, yes?

During good times high net worth shown on a balance sheet can certainly be comforting. It can even induce a feeling of pride: "Look at all that stuff I own!"

However, many of the assets on a construction pros balance sheet will, during down times, suddenly start acting like liabilities (not in the technical accounting sense but in the real-life sense). The truck, the handsomely remodeled office, the big shop and warehouse, the heavy equipment, the costly tools – they are eating up time and money for maintenance, insurance, taxes, and storage. Meanwhile, they are steadily depreciating in value. If bought with loans, they are gobbling up cash for the payments.

On paper and in accountant-speak, all that stuff you own might still be characterized as "assets." But in your day-to-day operations they are draining away your precious capital reserves. Rather than generating income, they have turned into burdens.

In construction, then, the balance sheet is a two-sided figure. Turned one way, it is a flattering friend. Turned the other, it is a voracious predator. Max's friend Oliver found that out in a hurry when his pleasing net worth, the eight houses he had under construction, abruptly became liabilities gobbling up the capital he had raised by mortgaging his home.

In construction, a balance sheet with only a few assets – just the equipment essential for the day-to-day operation of your company and a hefty amount of cash in reserve for hard times – is often preferable.

Need a dump truck now and then? Rent it, don't own it. Then it is someone else's problem during down times. Need bookkeeping? Outsource it rather than building space and installing computers for an in-house bookkeeper. In general, keep your company as unencumbered as possible with assets that can abruptly do an about-face and become burdens.

You want to achieve financial freedom? Train your brain to keep your eye on the prize. Head toward it by traveling light. Resist the thinking error that leads you to confuse ownership of a lot of non-essential stuff with real financial strength. Run a lean operation.

Keeping Purpose in Mind

Two major thinking problems that crop up in our world of construction are near-opposites of one another. Every skilled craftsman knows about the first: overthinking. I tended toward it as an apprentice carpenter.

I grew up in a family of scientists who earned their living by thinking things through very, very carefully. I brought the tendency with me when I was learning to cut lumber and fit sticks together. Before beginning even a simple task, I would attempt to visualize step-by-step exactly how I was going to accomplish it.

The lead carpenter I worked behind on a big condo project put a stop to my overthinking. It was not acceptable in work where time and money are so tightly linked. "Sometimes," the lead would tell me sardonically, "you gotta just do it." Buildings, not thought, were our product.

If we move from working as tradesmen to running our own businesses, we can fall into the reverse error: underthinking. Immersed in the details of running our companies, we have a hard time pulling back to take the long view.

Gino Wickman has, in the course of his long career as a consultant to entrepreneurs, observed many businesses. "Most business leaders," he reports in his book *Traction*, "spend most of their time overwhelmed, tired, buried in day-to-day routine, unable to see beyond tomorrow." They might be solving immediate problems. But they are not looking ahead. In other words, these "leaders" are not leading. How can you lead if you don't look up to see where you intend to go?

Why do we underthink? Perhaps because it such hard work. That's what *The Evening World* declared in an 1891 article about Thomas Edison, the inventor without whom we might not have our power tools: "Real thinking," said *The World* in a statement often repeated through the years, " is the hardest work in the world. That probably is why there is so little of it done."

Thinking is hard. Or maybe it's just that, especially for us construction guys, it's hard to slow yourself down enough to do it. The habits of mind we develop as tradesmen driving through production stand us in good stead as we churn through our daily management to-do list. But for the big decisions we need to be able to sit back and reflect. We need to pause and reflect whenever we are contacted about a possible project.

We must ask ourselves, Is this project right for us at this time? Will it fit together with our other projects? Do we have the capability to deliver it successfully? Will it take us in the direction we have intended to go? Are the owners folks we want to be involved with? Is their budget adequate? Will they be able to pay us enough to cover our costs of construction and the expenses of running our companies and also to make a profit?

Some years back, a representative of the founder of one of the largest technology companies in the United States called me about taking on a major remodel of his client's residence. My first impulse was to say "Yes!" and to plunge into the project. At first glance it looked like a step up into a world of opportunity beyond anything I had yet experienced. But I knew enough by then to pull back and reflect when temptation came along. I told the representative I needed to think about the project before giving him an answer.

I asked myself questions: Is this in fact a huge opportunity that can take my company to a new level? Or is it a potential monster that could swallow us whole? How does it fit in with our other commitments? How does it fit with our values?

Over the course of a few days and of moving back and forth between "just go for it, just do it" and "this project could overwhelm the company and set you back for years," I decided against it. The job was too far away for us to bring in our reliable team of trade partners. It was so big that it would consume us, pushing aside all other work for more than a year, and disconnect us from our usual network of clients.

Most important, it was too far outside the boundary of work that I thought was worth doing. I did not want to go in the direction of building additional luxury at huge residences whose construction and maintenance does so much damage to the environment. And I did not like the idea of working with a representative of the owner and having no chance to connect with and size up the man himself. I called the representative back, thanked him for considering us, and said no.

Making thoughtful decisions about taking on or passing up the projects that come knocking on your door is a good start toward that hard and crucial mental work. Another level of thought requires more effort. That is searching out and evaluating new directions for your company. You have to ask yourself: What other kinds of markets are out there? Which ones am I suited for? Should I try to break into them? How could I break into them?

If you are a residential builder can you and should you go after commercial work? Build for the Navy? Build for colleges? You must figure out and consider just what such work might involve that is different from the work you now do. You must ask yourself, Can I successfully bridge over to it? Can I break the transition down into manageable steps? What might be the benefits? What might be the costs? (Alas, all benefits seem to come with costs.) Is it the kind of work I want to be doing? Does it align with my larger purposes?

I have seen construction pros try out new markets. Their results have been mixed. One moved from residential remodeling to constructing new restaurants inside existing structures. He prospered. He had restaurant jobs going on major avenues all around his town.

Another residential builder accepted a few commercial jobs but found that he did not like doing them. They were too much about money and not enough about the other values that mattered to him, like the quality of relationships during a job. He preferred the much more personal work of building homes for families. He turned away from commercial. It did not take him where he wanted to go.

Purposeful thinking is likewise necessary for the cost-effective development of business systems. Impulsive moves won't cut it. You don't want to just snatch a product off the shelf without evaluating its costs versus its potential benefits. That hot new software that you are hearing about, will it actually increase your effectiveness? Or will it just add extra steps to your office procedures while burdening you with another monthly bill? Is your current home-based office becoming inadequate as your volume of work increases? Do you need to rent or buy commercial space? Or can you avoid that added burden by outsourcing more of your office work? That marketing program you are being encouraged to invest in by a persuasive consultant: Is it actually going to produce enough additional profit to justify its costs in time and money?

Every major aspect of a construction business requires consideration and reconsideration. It's so easy to duck away from the necessary reflection and turn instead to the next item on the to-do list, take the next phone call, or fight the latest fire. How do we correct against that temptation? How do we correct for underthinking and move forward purposefully?

The answer is straightforward. You make space for thinking. You make time for it. Wickman insists that if you want to effectively lead your company, you have to back off from the hustle and bustle and "escape the office on a regular basis" for quiet reflection. "Pick a one-hour block" each week he instructs. Think of it as "an appointment you schedule with yourself." Make the appointment and keep it without fail.

That is much like the solution I arrived at early in my career. I made the appointment with myself by writing the word "THINK" and circling it at regular intervals in my calendar. When thinking time came, I headed for a favorite coffee shop where they made good Americanos. I intended to enjoy one while I did my thinking. It was easier to overcome my resistance to slowing down and taking that time for reflection if I associated it with a treat.

It's essential, of course, when you head away from the hustle and bustle for an hour or two of thinking, to turn off your phone. You may also want to bring along a prompt to nudge your thoughts forward. My prompt was a card I pulled out of my wallet and read at the start of my hour with my Americano.

The card displayed a pyramid of values – maintaining integrity, using resources with care, being fair to everyone including myself, and a few more – that I try to live up to in my work. I would look over the values, attempt to sense any slippage in company practices, and consider opportunities going forward.

My mind would wander. But by the time the Americano was gone, I had sharpened my sense of purpose and grasped the actions needed to realize it. Yes, we would take on the project with the Zebra Design Studio. They'd be difficult in some ways, hovering over us, constantly asking for changes. But they were passionate about their work, responsive to questions, and honest. No, I would not buy a new truck to replace the GMC. Or at least not till I had crunched the numbers to determine if a new truck would be less costly over the next decade than keeping the GMC in good repair.

One thing I need to emphasize: By "keeping purpose in mind" I mean something different than the kind of business planning touted by certain business coaches and consultants. They insist on the necessity of plans: Five-year plans. Ten-year plans. Even longer plans. Typically, the plans call for hitting a series of financial targets along a timeline. Construction pros tune in to the consultants and echo their language. They speak proudly of their plans: Doubling revenue every year for five years. Going from 1 million the first year to 16 million in the fifth year. Increasing profit margins by *x* percentage over the next twelve months.

I am dubious about such plans. I am more inclined toward the kind of planning utilized by a certain world-class chess player. He was asked how he planned for his matches. He said he had no plan. Every time his opponent made a move, he faced a new problem. In response, he figured out his next move; but he did not plan beyond that.

The construction business, it seems to me, is slow-motion chess. Yes, you have to understand the contest you are engaged in. You must have a sense of the outcomes you hope to enjoy. You must have purpose, as obviously the chess player has a purpose, i.e., to win his games.

Your purpose may be to create an outstanding one-person company and hone your craft skills to the highest level possible. It may be to create a compact design/build firm that turns out excellent work from conceptual drawings through the last detail on the construction punch list. Maybe you aim to create a large company that posts its name on some of the most prominent projects around town. Maybe you want to develop a marketing machine that pulls in projects with high levels of profitability. Maybe you want to create a company that you can turn on and off at will so that you work half the year building and, during the other half, teach philosophy at Harvard or go fishing in England – as do a couple of general contractors I know.

But whatever your purpose, like the chess player, you will be working through constantly shifting terrain. You should understand that you must constantly adjust and recalibrate as you drive forward. Sometimes you can plan, but sometimes you must pivot.

You want to expand production as a custom home builder. You had your eye on a piece of land you could divide into lots for four houses. But interest rates are rising. A spec house you had just completed is not selling. Like the chess player, you realize you must create a new move to deal with the changes on the board. You rent the spec house, becoming a landlord for the first time, and hold off on the purchase of the land.

Or you had wanted to push your revenue over a million during the coming year. A severe recession sets in. You put aside revenue goals and focus instead on keeping your crew employed at whatever small jobs you can drum up. You intend to fight forward with them until the economy gives you a renewed opportunity for expansion.

You had begun to move aggressively into building and remodeling restaurants. A pandemic strikes. Restaurants are closing rather than contracting for construction work. But demand for home improvements begins to ramp up. You re-intensify your efforts to attract residential work. Soon the phone is ringing off the hook (as it was for residential builders around the country during the COVID-19 pandemic).

Attempting to move forward in accordance with the dictates of a business plan, rather than adjusting as circumstances require, can seriously compromise your long-term financial purposes. If you try to proceed too strictly according to plan, you may attempt growth when profitable growth is not possible. Instead of profit, you experience loss. That's the mistake Max's friend Oliver made. Following a plan in his head that dictated headlong growth, he rapidly expanded his volume rather than recalibrating as economic conditions demanded. You know how that worked out.

Navigating by too rigid a plan can cause you to jump into investments when you should not. Intent on marching toward financial freedom on a ten-year timeline, you invest in overpriced stocks or real estate. Instead, you should have been storing up capital while patiently waiting for a good moment to invest. You were imprisoned by your plan and unable to flexibly adjust to the changing economic and financial topography.

Pursuing cast-in-stone goals dictated by a business plan can even lead to misconceptions about yourself and your abilities. It can lead you to unduly celebrate your entrepreneurial genius when the economy is allowing you to hit targets. It can then cause you to make the reverse error of personalizing the events and seeing yourself as inadequate when you are being swept back by forces beyond your control.

Finding your way forward with purpose but also with flexibility is a better option in construction than trying to bull your way across a goal line before the clock runs out. It is not my place to tell you what your purpose should be. Whatever your purpose may be, you may find that it is difficult to stay on course. Distractions abound. Oddly, just being in business can itself be a distraction. You may find yourself becoming more interested in business than in the construction that is your business's product.

That can be dangerous. As your attention slips, so will the quality of the work you turn out. But a further step can be even worse: You may find your attention wandering to other kinds of businesses that you are not meant for. Gino Wickman warns of being "distracted by (supposed) opportunities that are wolves in sheep clothing." He cautions against "falsely assuming that because you are capable in one sort of business you can succeed at another."

I have seen distraction undermine the focus and purpose of capable construction pros. Some have recovered, some have not. The banker-turned-builder that I mentioned earlier set out to do outstanding work like that of the builders who inspired his move into construction. He put together a small company that enjoyed success building high-quality custom homes in a rapidly redeveloping urban area.

Then distraction hit. He became infatuated with the idea of creating a national homebuilding firm. As a first step, he began building housing tracts in outlying suburbs. The budgets feasible for tract work did not allow him to do the quality of work that had drawn him to construction in the first place. Fortunately, he suffered no crippling financial setbacks. He was able to unwind the tract operation and return to the custom work that fed his spirit.

Another builder set out to construct homes for families unable to afford even the lower-end tract houses available in his area. He succeeded, creating a new neighborhood and successfully selling all of his houses with satisfactory profit margins. But then, it seems, he got bored with the very thing he had proved himself so adept at. He wandered off to projects of a much different sort. He went bankrupt.

I could cite further examples. But instead let me bring Warren Buffett in here. Buffett, as you likely know, is famous as an investor. He is also a businessman. His company, Berkshire Hathaway, which is in the business of selecting and monitoring investments, has about the same number of employees as a midsize construction company. Buffett, too, warns about being distracted and becoming untethered from one's purpose. Any company, he says, can "stagnate because of hubris or boredom that causes the attention of managers to wander."

Rather than falling prey to inattention, we need to pay attention. We need to put aside distraction. We need to keep purpose in mind. My assumption is that if you are reading this book, part of your purpose is to achieve financial freedom. To do that, you will need capital. To acquire capital, you will need to understand profit. You will need to hone strategies for earning and protecting it.

PART TWO:
Building a Profit Engine

- The What and the Why of Profit
- Constructing Profit Opportunities
- Numbers
- Protecting Your Profit

The What and the Why of Profit

Bryan Uhler leads a homebuilding company in Washington State that was founded by his father, Tim. Bryan speaks appreciatively of his father's values of frugality and modesty and of one particularly important lesson his father taught him about the construction business. It's one we've alluded to earlier when emphasizing that owner's pay is part of overhead. It's so important it's worth our while to give it a longer look here. That lesson, as Bryan's father put it to him, is this: *Wages are not profit. Profit is not wages. Don't mix them up.*

Bryan's father had learned that lesson early. He entered construction from the number-crunching side of the business, whereas many of us enter from the trade side, with little knowledge of business. He understood: Your wages (or salary, also called "draw,") are *what you get paid* for work you do for a company, even if it is your own company. Profit is *what a company earns* after paying all costs and expenses for the labor, material, and trade partners involved in the construction of projects and for running the business – including pay the owner takes for their work in the field or office.

When Tim Uhler started his own homebuilding company, he always paid himself a wage. Tim did a lot of work for his company, from sweeping floors to keeping the books. If he had not done that work himself, he would have had to pay someone else to do it.

He understood that the cost of the work, whoever did it, had to be recognized in his company's accounting records. It had to be subtracted from his company's revenue. And the only way to make sure that was done was to cut himself a check and record it in the records.

He grasped this key point: If he failed to subtract the cost, he would be fooling himself into thinking his company was more profitable than it actually was. That's why he paid himself and deducted his pay from company revenue on the way to figuring the company profits. He taught the practice to his son.

As we shall discuss further along in this chapter, a company needs its earnings as much as you need your pay. Without earnings, it has as little chance of surviving as you would have without pay. Unfortunately, failing to separate owner's pay and company profit, even thinking they are the same thing – and therefore not being able to accurately assess the profitability of their companies – is typical for guys new to the construction business. For some, the confusion lasts for a long while.

A superb lead carpenter, who worked in my company for two decades before going on his own some years ago, got off to a particularly painful start. He was doing remodel jobs, charging his clients an hourly rate for his labor, and providing all material on the projects at cost. "I am doing okay," he would tell me when I stopped by his projects to see how things were going.

Then he disclosed his numbers to me. They were horrible. His financial compensation was far less than he had enjoyed in our company. He was charging his customers the base wage he had received as a company employee. But gone was his share of the company's annual profits. Gone was his medical plan. Gone were all his other benefits, from the company's contribution to his social security account to travel allowances (not to mention company-provided donuts and coffee).

Now he had to buy his own tools and crew supplies, from pencils to blades and bits, that were formerly supplied by the company. He had to work long hours off the jobsite at estimating and the other management work required by his start-up operation. For those costs and hours, he was not collecting a cent.

The math was ugly. He was charging his clients thirty dollars an hour, collecting $1,200 for forty hours a week of on-site work (30 × 40 = 1,200). But including his off-site work to run his new business, he was working sixty hours, which brought his hourly pay down to twenty dollars an hour (1,200 ÷ 60 = 20).

Out of that meager pay, he had to cover the out-of-pocket costs of being in business – not only for construction tools but also for his office supplies and equipment. All said and done, his take-home pay was, at most, around sixteen dollars an hour – less than a third of his total compensation package when we worked together. That is what he was calling "doing okay."

Fortunately, he soon realized he was not cut out to be in business for himself. When clients groaned about the costs of their projects, he could not bring himself to charge them what I had charged our customers for his on-site work, much less enough to cover his overhead and provide a profit to his business. He gave up general contracting and found employment with another company. Last I heard, he had established himself in that company as "the indispensable project manager."

Other builders make the reverse of the mistake made by my former lead carpenter. They don't mistake pay for profit. Instead they treat profit as pay. They charge their customers enough to pay themselves market rates for their work, both on and off their job sites, to recapture their out-of-pocket expenses for company operations, and to make a profit. But they treat everything beyond what it takes them to pay their company's bills as personal pay.

That's easy enough to do. If you own and run a private company, just where you draw the line between pay and profit is strictly your call. It's your choice as to just how you divide up the money that remains after you have met payroll, paid your subs and suppliers, and covered all the costs of running your company. But if you stick too much of that money in your pocket as take-home pay, leaving little to nothing for your company, you won't like the long-term consequences.

A builder I know well told me, "I think I have been paying myself too much." He surely had been. He had been taking nearly every dime his company earned beyond costs and expenses and ladling it onto his plate as pay, then spending it. He and his wife, though they had no children, built a huge house, regularly traveled abroad, and drove luxurious vehicles. Then a severe recession struck. Work stopped coming in. The builder's only prospective job got hung up in the permitting process. He had set aside virtually nothing of his profits for such contingencies. With little cash in reserve, he became terrified that he was not going to be able to pay his business bills or even his mortgage.

He managed to hold on through the recession. A few years later he was nearing sixty and was worrying about retirement. That, too, was realistic. He was facing a dismal future. He still owed a lot on his mortgage and had yet to build up adequate cash reserves for his company. Because he had treated all profit as pay and consumed it, he had not been able to make the investments that support a life free from money anxieties during his senior years.

"Eli," as I will call him here, had greater success coming to terms with the pay/profit issue than either my former lead or my spendthrift builder friend. He arrived at success due to a lesson acquired at the school of hard knocks. After being employed for a couple of decades as a project manager, Eli had started his own company.

He did make the typical beginner's error of underpaying himself. But he soon realized he was collecting far less total compensation than he had received from his former boss. Gradually, from one job to the next, he increased his labor rate.

All along he expected to hit customer resistance. But he never did. Because he did good work and was reliable, he remained in demand even as he raised his charges. Within a few years he had climbed back up the compensation ladder. He got back to the level he had been at when he ran jobs for his old employer – at least for his work on his jobsites if not for the work of running his business.

Next, he learned to include enough in his charges to clients to also recapture his out-of-pocket costs for managing his compact business. After a few more years, he was even earning enough from his projects to provide pay for his work off the jobsite as well as on it. He felt fine about all those charges. He was getting reimbursed for all his costs and expenses and all of his time. He was, in his mind, getting what he deserved to get.

At that point, Eli hit the wall. He felt uneasy about charging something additional, something more for profit. Six years into running his own business, he was negotiating for the largest project of his career, the complete renovation and expansion of a large Victorian home. He completed a thorough estimate and totaled up his figures. They appalled him. One million and two hundred thousand dollars and change! He was worried. Was he overcharging the nice young couple who had entrusted him with the reconstruction of their home? Was he ripping them off?

Eli called me. I reviewed his estimate. His numbers for construction costs and overhead looked accurate, I told him. But where was the charge for profit?

He shook his head. He wasn't charging for profit. "How can I?" he exclaimed. He was already going to make a fortune! Just look at the huge amount in the estimate for his compensation as lead carpenter and project manager on the year-long project. He was uneasy about asking for even more. It wasn't that he was afraid of losing the job. He just felt guilty about asking for profit in addition to a year's worth of pay for his work on and off the jobsite.

Earlier in my career I likely have would gone along with him. During those years the saying that "money is the root of all evil" rang true to me. I viewed profit making as an unsavory capitalist tendency. By the time I reviewed Eli's estimate, I had moved on from those sentiments.

I had come to appreciate that it was often a *lack* of money that caused evil – hunger, misery, deprivation, even criminality. And it was surely lack of money that caused one construction company after another to go bust when they hit hard times or underbid a job and had nothing set aside from past profits to see them through.

"No!" I told Eli. "You are not charging enough if you are not including profit in your bid for the job."

I did not offer Eli the justification for profit that I often hear – namely, that it is a reward you somehow are automatically entitled to for taking the risks of being in business. I've never been happy with that cliché. It is flat-out incorrect. You do not deserve profit just because you are taking risk. In fact, if you take a stupid risk, you should (and likely will) get punished, not rewarded. The cliché does not do justice to the reality and the necessity of profit in construction.

The reality is that there are three kinds of costs in construction. There are your direct costs for on-site work by you, your crew, and your trade partners. There are the overhead expenses from computer ink to office furniture that we've been at pains to enumerate. And there are what I call "profit costs."

You are all but certain to repeatedly experience profit costs during your career. They are the unanticipated costs, arriving out of the blue, that put the great majority of construction companies out of business within their first decade. I have identified several dozen profit costs. The list is included in the "Resources" section at the end of this book. In the glossary you will find a definition for "profit costs" that contrasts them to what are commonly called "contingencies."

Profit costs can arise from a project before construction begins, while it's in progress, and after, even long after, it is completed. Profit costs are the losses you take as a result of unexpectedly severe weather that slows production at a jobsite, from clients balking at legitimate change order charges, from subs going out of business during a job with their work half done, from lawsuits you get caught up in even when your work has nothing to do with the central issue in the suit, and from tool theft and recessions and embezzlement.

Profit costs can arise from mega-events far beyond your control such as pandemics and cyberattacks causing a widespread breakdown in computers.

Other profit costs arise closer to home. They result when building departments enforce special requirements that you did not know about. Profit costs pile up when you get involved with an obsessive client who has little construction knowledge but badgers your crew about construction details. Or when designers give your crew and trade partners bad specs and details.

It was that last type of profit cost that ambushed Eli at his big job and taught him his lesson about the need for profit.

Eli had carefully installed exterior siding exactly in accordance with the specifications and details in the architect's plans. The siding failed, both leaking and warping. The architect disclaimed responsibility, though the failure appeared to be the result of his specifications.

The owner threatened Eli, who in turn engaged a hard-charging construction expert to help him defend himself. After an afternoon of contentious debate, a compromise was reached. The owners agreed to not sue. Eli agreed to remove and replace the failed siding. He spent a month and a half doing the work. He did that without pay.

After being hit with that profit cost, Eli no longer had trouble including profit in his bids. He now understood that profit was not his personal pay, but pay for his company. He began charging for profit and setting it aside as a buffer against possible future profit costs.

Profit costs are like wolves circling your campfire in the night. Now and then one gets through and takes a bite out of your hide. If you are an unusually attentive and capable (and lucky) manager of your business, you may be able to keep the wolves mostly at bay. You will be able to retain a good deal of your profit. If so, you best not pile it all onto your plate as your personal pay.

Your priority for profit (or to be exact, after-tax profit) must be to build up those cash reserves necessary to see your company through hard times. Your company will need the reserves to cover whatever profit costs arrive out of the blue. Any profit that remains after you have topped up the reserves, you can share out between yourself and your loyal, long-term employees.

Just what you do with your share of profit – that's a personal decision. You may want to use it for immediate gratification and increase your level of personal consumption. You may choose to go the pickup-truck-millionaire route and put it entirely into those investments that enable financial freedom. Or do something of both. Your call.

Few construction companies make substantial profits, especially over the long term. In fact, the profit picture for construction as a whole is so dismal it brings a question to mind: Is construction a "not-for-profit industry"? I tossed that question to my audience once when I was invited to speak to a group of seasoned builders. I had not intended to make a joke. But they burst into laughter. They knew from experience exactly what I meant.

I expanded on the idea in a side commentary in my book on estimating and bidding. The heart of it is this: Reported average profitability for small- and medium-size light-frame builders (remodelers and builders of homes and smaller commercial projects) runs about 4 percent during *good* years. Factor in down years, and the average drops even lower.

Even those modest numbers are, however, for the companies who managed to stay in business. The numbers for the companies that collapsed are not included in the averages. That's like tallying up the results of a war but not counting the dead. Factor in the dead, and the profit levels for light-frame construction as a whole appear to be negligible at best and quite possibly nonexistent.

Leslie Shiner has observed the not-for-profit problem during the many years she provided accounting services and financial education to construction pros. Earlier in her career she worked with nonprofits. When she switched over to our world, she saw that the profitability picture for construction pros was much like that of her previous clients. Like the nonprofits, they did not generate profit.

The difference, of course, was that they were supposed to and needed to make a profit. Instead of being nonprofits with legal status as such, Leslie's construction clients simply ran not-for-profit businesses. Operating a construction company as a not-for-profit is not likely to work out well for its owner in the long run. In order for your business to survive (or at least to do better than to barely survive), you need to create opportunities to make a profit. You need to put into place the systems and practices that will allow you to retain that profit.

Constructing Profit Opportunities

There's a saying in construction: "You make your money when you sign the contract for a project." There's truth in that. A good contract establishes the possibility of covering your costs, earning owner's pay, and enjoying a company profit.

A question arises: How do you acquire those contracts? A further question: Just what practices must you build into your operation so that you actually cover costs, earn your pay, and realize profits? We will discuss a range of possibilities: Targeting the right range of projects. Charging for estimating and other preconstruction work as well as for construction itself. And honing efficiency on and off the jobsite. But let's begin with marketing and sales, the necessary initial steps to winning those good contracts.

Since I first became a builder, I have encountered two schools of thought about marketing. The first teaches you to let your words do the talking. When I was starting out, construction pros got their words out via brochures, yellow page ads, and trade shows. They published advice columns in newspapers or magazines. Some tried cold calling door-to-door. These days such methods have been in good part replaced by digital word delivery. Now the go-to media are websites loaded with photography and testimonials, blogs, newsletters delivered via email, and social media postings.

Certain marketing firms specialize in helping construction companies build digital programs. They call the programs "inbound marketing." It will, they claim, draw customers who are already "inbound," i.e., browsing on the web in search of construction services. By contrast, the old way of marketing is said to be like performing music on the sidewalk, hoping someone will pause to listen.

The difference between the old and the new may not be so stark as the vendors of digital marketing want us to believe. When you buy a display ad in the construction section of a weekly newspaper, post an ad in the yellow pages, or put up a jobsite sign, the people who take notice will largely be those browsing around for construction services. Are they not as "inbound" as someone deciding to click on your website?

Whatever the case, with both the old and the new media, you are letting your words do the talking. The second school of thought about marketing urges you to let your actions – your work – do the talking. You produce the best construction you are capable of. You strive to get better at producing it with every project you deliver. You deliver the work at a competitive price. You treat clients and their properties with respect.

Your performance thrills your clients. They, along with the design professionals you work with, become the marketing division of your company. They recommend you to their friends and colleagues. Your phone beeps. Potential new customers are calling or texting.

The guys who emphasize letting their work do the talking believe what one of my mentors taught me: "You are better off taking care of one old client than chasing ten new prospects."

Even if you largely count on your work to do the talking, you may wish to invest in other marketing. Minimally, these days, you will want a low-cost website that makes it easy for prospective customers to find you and that intensifies their interest in your company. If you go beyond that, make sure that your additional investment in marketing is producing more in additional profit than it is burdening you with cost. That might seem a maxim so obvious it isn't worth the sentence I just gave it. Yet I have long seen it ignored.

Decades ago, I read an article about marketing by the chief executive of a prominent company that provided business education and consulting to construction companies. I analyzed the numbers in the article. My conclusion: The recommended outlay for marketing was not likely to produce enough additional profit to pay for the marketing. Yes, you read that right. The marketing was going to cost more than it earned back.

Fast-forwarding to the present, I encounter parallel dubious urgings from one of the new agencies promoting digital marketing to the construction industry. They advocate, without explanation, that clients spend 1–1.5 percent of their total revenue on marketing. That's huge! It's a sizable portion of the profit retained by construction companies.

In order to promote itself, this particular agency trumpets its effectiveness at increasing leads and volume of work for its clients. It is, however, all but silent about the relationship of its marketing program to profitability. It does not address the central question: To what extent does the increase in leads and volume lead to improved financial performance? Volume is of little worth if it does not come with profitability. In fact, it may just put your company further out on a limb, increasing your potential liabilities without providing the capital reserves you may need to discharge them.

Your investment in marketing must be monitored for effectiveness. That's simple enough to do. When you get a lead, create a brief record about the project and client. (If you want to take a look at my record sheet for leads, it is available to you without charge in my article "Bid Wisely, Estimate Accurately" at *JLC* online.) Label the lead by source – past client, friend, trade partner or marketing. Track your results on the jobs arising out of those different sources. Determine whether you are actually signing contracts for the leads attracted through marketing. Determine how much time you had to spend to get to those contracts. Calculate what your financial results are if you build the projects. Compare your results with projects that come your way via references.

You may find that projects obtained through marketing burden you with more preconstruction time and cost and return less to your bottom line than projects from references. Possibly, the investment in marketing will still be worthwhile if it enables you to sufficiently expand your base of satisfied clients or to break into a new market. Otherwise, you will be investing in a vehicle that is taking you backward, not further along the road to financial freedom.

Whatever marketing you do, you must follow it up with effective sales calls. You must encounter your prospective clients and move with them toward that good contract. Effective – and ethical – selling is, to my way of thinking, straightforward. You begin a sale by talking on the phone with a prospective client, particularly about desired scope of work and budget. If it seems it might be worthwhile, you meet with the client.

Then you *listen*. As my mentor in sales taught me, "That meeting is about them, not about you." So, you *listen* for as long as they need you to. You candidly answer their questions. Then, as they wind down, you offer them your thoughts about their project. You try to provide them with information that will be useful no matter who they choose to work with.

If the clients and their project seem like a good fit for you, you ask if they would like to hear about your company. If so, you give them a brief account – one you have worked out and practiced so that you can offer it concisely and clearly. You lay out for the client your company's strengths – what experts on selling call "points of separation" between yourself and your competition.

If you are just starting out, your primary point of separation might be that you are on the job every workday, personally making sure each detail is right. Later in your career, you may stress that you run an employee centered company. The result, you explain, is that your crew and trade partners stick with you. The same folks who completed projects on time and on budget for past clients will be serving the new client.

That is selling as I understand it. You are building trust by practicing what is esteemed as "social selling," i.e., socially responsible selling. You do selling as learning and teaching, not manipulation. You are trying to understand your clients' needs and provide them with useful ideas. Manipulation and slick sales tactics are not necessary if you are selling good work at a fair price. As Nassim Taleb, best known for his writings on probability and uncertainty but also a keen analyst of financial and business issues, has written, "Marketing beyond conveying information is a sign of insecurity."

As part and parcel of marketing, you consider (and repeatedly reconsider) the types of project opportunities you want to say yes to and those you want to decline. Some marketing and sales consultants advise construction pros to "find their sweet spot." Determine the types of jobs that are most profitable for you and concentrate on winning those kinds of jobs, they urge. There's value in the advice. It won't hurt to go after jobs of the type you know to be profitable – and that you enjoy!

On the other hand, concentrating on a narrow range of jobs could become boring. And it can lead to overspecialization. Overly specialized organisms that get along in only a limited range of conditions tend not to survive. A certain construction company specialized in building restaurants. It thrived during the restaurant boom in its city. Then the COVID-19 pandemic struck. Restaurants closed down en masse. The construction company folded, too. Its website disappeared. A message at its old phone number informed callers the office was shut until further notice.

Better advice might be, "Know your sweet spot. Work it. *Gradually* enlarge it." Note the emphasis on "gradually." Do not follow in the footsteps of the builder who was good at bath and kitchen remodeling, and then, against the advice of wiser heads, jumped to contracting for construction of a large custom home. He went bankrupt.

Instead, travel a path like the one taken by an Australian builder over the course of several decades. He began by doing small repairs and minor improvement jobs. Then a step at a time – including a step backward to installing fences when the economy slumped – he worked his way through building additions, houses, smaller multi-unit developments, then larger ones. Last I heard, he had developed a pair of fifteen-story condo towers.

Among the best methods of constructing profitability: Deliver exceptionally good work. Deliver it with really good service. In other words, in business school-speak, "Build a brand."

Construction pros have not enjoyed the increased esteem that has been accorded other entrepreneurs over the last half century. Too often, tradespeople and the companies that employ them are looked down upon. But for all that, the construction pros who provide exceptional quality are held in high regard by their clients. Their clients hold parties to honor their pro when a project is complete. They thank the friend or acquaintance who recommended them. And they, in turn, enthusiastically recommend them to friends.

To get to the point where your work delights and attracts clients – that it has a certain charismatic quality, that your company is a respected "brand" – you have to put in the hard miles. You have to learn to produce the exceptionally good work. Just about every construction pro seems to think they already do. My observation has been that few do (though a good number turn out what can be called "decent" work).

Producing and maintaining quality takes relentless effort. One builder, bent on ensuring quality down to the last detail, created a checklist of quality standards for all trades that worked on their projects. The checklist covers several hundred items. It is always expanding. A quality control officer in the company makes sure all standards are met at every project. They are high standards. They are not the marginal standards put forth by a major homebuilders association that are designed to provide builders with a defense for mediocre work.

Fernando Pagés Ruiz, a veteran builder and author of *Building the Affordable House,* invented another way to exercise quality control. He tracked problems and failures at his projects by categories such as framing, plumbing, and windows. Soon he was able to see where his quality was falling short and hitting him with profit costs.

Pagés Ruiz made the changes necessary to hold onto profit. He saw that costs were piling up due to leakage in the inexpensive windows he had been using to stay within the tight budgets for his highly affordable houses. He moved to higher-grade windows. Failures sharply dropped off. Profits stayed with him.

Such controls are powerful. They are not enough. Because installation is the primary determinant of quality, you must hire people who insist on doing good work, who would do good work even if no one was ever going to inspect it. How can you do that? One way: Interview prospective employees at one of your projects. Choose a project where the quality from jobsite maintenance to the crispness of the installed work is obvious.

Observe whether the interviewee responds to, or better yet, can specifically identify the quality. If yes, maybe they are a good candidate. If no, the chances are lower. (Interviews are at best first impressions and first impressions often prove mistaken.) You'll know soon after they begin working whether they can actually meet your standards. If they don't, release them early during their probation period and try again.

Once you are sure they can, position them as their own quality control managers. Give them articles and videos about the work they do. Leave it to them to construct their own quality control procedures. You will get results.

The book *Small Giants* tells the story of a manufacturing company that once did its quality checks at the point product came off its assembly line. It changed to giving responsibility for quality control to people working on the line. Both quality and efficiency shot up.

Remember the lesson from our discussion of employee centered companies: Workers, certainly the workers you want to employ, desire responsibility and autonomy. Give it to them. They will respond.

My crews demanded autonomy and took responsibility. They were responsible for quality. I was the quality control officer, inspecting jobs thoroughly to provide backup verification of quality. It was a great job that gave me joy. I rarely found anything wrong. I found a great deal to admire.

High-quality work enables construction of another profit possibility: cultivating "customers for life," to use a phrase popular in the remodeling world. If you have wowed a customer the first time you worked for them, there is a good chance they will turn to you for their next project. At least they are likely to do that if you make sure they know you are available. You can't assume they do. I learned that from an unhappy experience.

I was sitting in my truck enjoying lunch one afternoon. A woman passed by. We recognized each other. She and her husband had been clients of mine years earlier. Building for them had been a good experience. They were friendly, appreciative, and paid promptly. When the woman saw me in my truck, she blurted, "David, you're still a builder! We thought you had gone to grad school. Oh goodness, I wish we had known."

She'd recently had a horrible time remodeling her kitchen and other spaces in her home. The builder was a slob. Many days he left her house a mess. Other days he did not show up at all. The project, which should have taken six months max, had gone on for two years.

Her project would have been mine had I taken the trouble to let her know I was still in business. Moral of the story: Make certain that those past customers you'd like to work for again do not forget you or assume you are gone. At the very least, send them an appreciative note annually, perhaps at Thanksgiving, expressing how fortunate you feel to have worked with them.

David Lupberger, a former remodeler turned business coach, encourages a more active practice. He notes that the end of a project can be "just the beginning of your relationship with the client." He suggests arranging to visit clients regularly to discuss their needs for repairs, renovations, or remodels. By staying in touch with clients and taking care of their maintenance and small projects, Lupberger says, you will ensure that they have not forgotten you when they get to their next big one. Additionally, Lupberger emphasizes, the small jobs will provide a reliable income stream that will help you get through recessions when larger jobs are hard to come by.

When we stay in touch with past clients, we increase our chances of cultivating customers for life. We construct opportunities for profitability. We also enjoy the affirmation of their enduring trust.

Cultivating future work is one path to constructing profitability. Another is increasing the profitability of the work you are already doing. Most simply, you can raise your charges for profit during periods of high demand for construction. You may encounter resistance. However, if you are a reliable builder who produces high-quality work, chances are, as we noted in "Thought Remodeling," it won't be coming from potential customers. It will come from within. A voice in your head will say, "If I try to charge more, I won't get any jobs."

Countless builders have encountered that voice. Some have discovered it was in their head, not out in the world. How do you determine which is the case for you? Raise your profit charges in small increments. If you continue to win good contracts, then you were your problem.

You will find additional opportunity to increase profitability from the work you are already doing by looking for leaks within your operations, particularly those that take the form of wasted time. As I was taught at the beginning of my carpentry apprenticeship, time equals money in construction. Plug the time leaks at your projects and in your office and money stays inside the company as profit.

The leaks and their elimination can be represented by what I think of as "the parable of the carpenter's pencil." For years, I had preferred the traditional flat carpenter's pencil for rough work. When my pencil dulled, I would sharpen it to a point. A veteran carpenter suggested I sharpen it instead to a chisel like edge. Took less time and produced two points, one at each corner of the "chisel," rather than just a single point, he explained.

I figured I had been sharpening my pencil about every half hour, i.e., sixteen times during a workday, with each sharpening taking about a minute. All told, I had been spending sixteen minutes a day sharpening, Now, sharpening to a chisel-like edge and getting two points rather than just one, I would be sharpening eight times a day and saving eight minutes a day.

If you care to do the math, you'll see that the daily savings of eight minutes adds up to thirty-two hours in a year. At $80 per hour in carpenter's compensation (for wages plus benefits and employment taxes), that thirty-two hours costs $2,560. That's a nice chunk of additional profit for improving pencil sharpening.

You can find many such unglamorous opportunities to reduce time leaks at jobsites. You can find many more in your office. Joe Stoddard is a management consultant who helps builders streamline their operations. He reports inspecting offices where *fully half of the processes add no value* – are just leaking away time – and a great many more need trimming.

Would Joe spot that kind of inefficiency in your office? When a bill or receipt arrives in the office, how many times is it handled? How many handlings could be eliminated? When you or someone else in your office has questions for a project manager, do they call immediately when a question arises and therefore interrupt the project manager repeatedly during the day? Or do they consolidate questions into one call? I know a project manager who complains of incessantly being interrupted by calls from the company office. (That company is notorious for inefficiency. It is virtually unable to win a job when the client is seeking competitive bids.)

If you can do something in ten steps, why do it in twenty? Stoddard asks. Good question. If you can do it in one, why in two? If you don't get a benefit from doing it, why do it at all?

I have a personal favorite method of constructing profitability within existing work. That is getting paid for estimating. There are no free estimates. Someone pays for them. You do, with your time, if you do your estimates personally. You do, with your cash, if you hire somebody to do them. Alternately, your client pays for them. If you have been paying for them, and you shift to having your clients pay you for estimating, you have created profitability that did not exist before. You do that without having to grow your company's volume.

Would you like to make the shift but are a bit hesitant? Begin by charging for the time it takes you to estimate the cost of change orders. Ease into that by providing in your contract that the first half-dozen hours for change order production will be free. After that, you charge. Once you are comfortable with that step, you can work your way to charging professional rates for your estimates and other preconstruction work.

Forty years ago, the idea of charging for an estimate for construction was virtually unheard of. The public had been conditioned to believe, as a potential client once said to me, that construction contractors were "supposed to provide free estimates."

I ended the phone call from that client promptly. By that time, I had been charging for estimates and related preconstruction work for many years. I had developed a presentation for potential clients that laid out all the benefits of a thorough, accurate, and transparent estimate. It was a good investment, I emphasized. It enabled analysis that would turn up opportunities for reducing cost while maintaining quality. It would enable the clients to build the best possible project for their available budget. The savings the analysis would generate would likely far exceed my charges for preconstruction work. Clients accepted my proposal. Charging for preconstruction work became my standard practice.

My practice is part of a movement – it may have even been the beginning of the movement – away from free, so-called "competitive bidding." About fifteen years after I began giving talks on "beyond bidding for free," the American Institute of Architects published a manual titled "Integrated Project Management." It urges architects to form a team with the owner, the engineers, and the builder at the outset of design rather than completing their drawings and seeking free bids.

The movement has spread beyond the United States. Duayne Pearce, an Australian builder, has become an apostle for the movement in his country. "Builders should be paid for their time," he insists. "Charge for your quotes. Don't be victimized by people just shopping around for a low price. Charging for your preconstruction estimating and related work will make people value it more."

All around the United States, construction pros now charge for generating estimates. Dennis Dixon, an Arizona homebuilder, refuses to give even a ballpark estimate without charge. Jared Gossett, a builder in Austin, Texas, says, "There's nothing wrong with spending an hour or two to see whether a client, you, and the project are a good fit. But after that you are moving into providing professional services."

A construction manager from Tennessee asks, "If a designer just hands you plans and asks for an estimate, why would you do that? Hell, even car mechanics have figured out that customers have to pay for a diagnostic."

One caveat: The Tennessee construction manager also says builders "deserve to get paid for their estimating work because they are professionals." I don't think so. You deserve to get paid for the work only if you do it well.

Unfortunately, many construction pros are unable (or unwilling) to produce estimates deserving of pay. Their estimates are woefully short of "professional." They are badly organized, skimpy, and inaccurate. They are based on guesswork, not accurate and complete quotes from suppliers and trade partners and reliable records of labor productivity. Worse, they deliberately conceal overhead and profit markups from the clients who are paying for the estimates.

Charging clients for estimating and other preconstruction work brings responsibilities beyond those of competitive bidding. You can't deliberately conceal key numbers to serve your own interests. Owners will be relying upon your numbers to make major decisions about the use of their financial resources. If you want to be paid for the work – thereby constructing a new profit center for your company – you must learn to get the numbers right. And they must be transparent so owners can clearly see where their costs lie.

Numbers

Construction demands a broad range of capabilities. If you work on job sites, you need athletic ability. You need to be able to move quickly, gracefully, safely. You need good hand-eye coordination and motor skills. You must become capable of visualization, developing the capacity to stare off into thin air and see in three dimensions how something not yet built can be put together.

For construction management and leadership, you best have social skills. You should be able to communicate clearly and effectively. You must learn to encourage and motivate others, to keep their spirits up during tough days and months and to support them in celebrating their successes.

Crucially, you must be good with numbers. Day in and day out, hour by hour, in construction you deal with numbers. At project sites you, or your crew and trade partners, constantly measure, count, and calculate. In order to win projects in the first place, you bid and estimate, fluently using math to figure quantity and cost. Once you have won a project and it is underway, you must track the dollars due for your work and the dollars spent to construct it. All along, the costs of running your company and its earnings have to be monitored. In short, you must attend to accounting.

The use of numbers at the job site we will leave to the many good books about carpentry and other trades. Here, in this book about reaching financial freedom, we want to focus first on the essentials of estimating and bidding. Then we will turn to accounting for *management* purposes (not for taxes, as that is best handled by you and your accountant).

Other than construction itself, estimating and bidding are arguably the most important tasks that your business performs.

You might turn out beautifully crafted work and be a good leader. You might have a bang-up marketing program. You may be a whiz at sales. Those skills will not serve you well if you are not good at estimating and bidding. They could even be counterproductive. You may sell jobs you'll lose your shirt on because you woefully underestimate them. Financial anxiety will then wipe away the joy you can experience from building. It's a real drag working with the worry that you are losing money on a job.

Estimating and bidding are not the same thing. We will look at them separately.

"Estimating," says Ian Schwandt, a construction veteran with substantial experience at estimating, "is like a dart game." For each round, he explains, you get three darts. One is for material costs. A second is for trade partner bids. The third is for labor by your crew. To achieve an acceptable score, you have to hit somewhere in the bull's-eye with all three darts. As Ian sees it, with the darts for material costs and trade partners, you are standing about two feet from the target. You don't have to do much more than reach out and stick the dart in the center of the target.

For materials, you begin by making an accurate count of all the material you will need for a job. With counting complete, and waste factors added, you write out your totals and send them to your suppliers with requests for written quotes (sales tax and delivery included). You don't settle for verbal quotes. If they are wrong, or you got them wrong, your supplier likely won't honor them.

When the written quotes come back, you've got reliable numbers for material. You've stuck the first dart in the bull's-eye. Maybe you did not hit it dead center. But across many jobs, if you are thorough, while you may be a little high on one job and a little low on another, there's a good chance you'll average out close to right on the money.

For trade partner bids, the essential steps are equally straightforward. You send a complete copy of the plans and the specs for the job to each trade partner. (How gloriously easy and inexpensive that is now in this era of PDFs, compared to the old days when paper plans had to be printed and distributed.) Along with the plans, you give each trade partner an "Included/Not Included" form. You will find a sample of my form in the "Tools" section at the back of this book. I have heard from readers that it has helped them. So please take a look at it.

You will see that the form requires – and this is crucial – a trade partner to alert you to any work *regularly performed by their trade that is not included in their bid*. If they don't alert you that an item is not included, then they are responsible for it.

Use of the form can largely eliminate a chronic problem, namely items of work falling between the trades. For example, you may see that your sheet metal, plumbing, and roofing subs are all excluding roof jacks. You ask one of them to add jacks to their bid. With no work falling between trades, you will get into the bull's-eye for trade partner work, too.

The third dart, for work by your own crew, is the tough one. Some construction estimators seem to be standing not two feet but about a hundred yards from the target when they throw the third dart. They miss so badly they have come to see estimating as hopeless. They'll mutter, "Estimating is art; you won't know what's in the picture till it is done. You can't know what a project will cost till its complete." Or "It's a crapshoot."

Those are lame excuses. We know they are because other construction pros consistently land all three darts within the bull's-eye. Some, to be sure, have taken a relatively easy path. They hardly make use of employees in the field. They have almost all on-site work from excavation to painting done by trade partners. Thereby, they have largely offloaded the challenge of estimating to their trade partners. The only labor they have to calculate is supervision by an in-house production manager and maybe a laborer or two. They even contract out final detailing.

Other estimators are very good at estimating costs for labor by their crews as well as for material and trade partner work. While they may run high on some jobs and low on others, they come reasonably close with their labor estimates. And over time, their highs and lows average out. Overall, they stay within the bull's-eye even with that third dart. I am one such estimator.

I have accomplished my accuracy at labor estimating by building up records of crew hours for tasks from foundation forming through door hardware installation. If you have read my other books, you have already seen my method. I apologize for the redundancy. But I have found the method so valuable, I want to share it again.

The records are not for gross costs such as the cost of all framing for an addition. You can't use the cost of framing one addition to accurately forecast the framing of a different addition by different crew.

The cost records are for particular items: Hours per foot for forming a T-footing foundation for a one-story house. Hours per sheet for laying subfloor at a second-story addition. Hours per piece for installing baseboard of a certain height and profile.

A sample of the form I use for my records is included in the "Tools" section of this book. As you can see, when a form is filled out, it records the conditions, such as access and weather, under which an item of work took place. It describes the crew that did the work. It describes the owner and designer. At its bottom line, it reports the crew's productivity. For example, a form could tell you that your crack crew framed 320 feet of 2x6 walls at a rate of one-half person-hour per foot on a job with these conditions: good access; a responsive designer; and an owner who contributed to high crew morale by, among other appreciative gestures, serving them coffee and homemade pastries every day (as did one of my favorite clients).

To land your three darts, you will need more than labor productivity records, Included/Not included forms from your trade partners, and written supplier quotes. Among other critical items: A methodical site inspection procedure. A keen eye for the intangible costs in a project, especially access. A well-designed estimating spreadsheet that doubles as a checklist and thereby helps ensure you do not overlook items in a job. Develop it all, and you can regularly hit the bull's-eye with all three darts. (In "Resources" you will see a reference to *Nail Your Numbers*, my book on estimating and bidding. It will take you deep into the how-to and refer you to other sources of guidance.)

There is another sort of challenge you may encounter in estimating: what Paul Eldrenkamp calls your fear-driven "inner underestimator." The underestimator suffers, Eldrenkamp declares, "from those chronic weaknesses shared by so many of us contractors: need for approval and fear of rejection, empathy for the client, doubts about self-worth, lack of confidence that you can replace this job if you lose it to a low bidder. We don't charge enough because we are afraid to charge enough."

The best remedy for fear, Eldrenkamp suggests, is knowledge. "If you know your numbers cold, you are less likely to convince yourself that they are too high and pare something off your estimate."

Exactly. That is why I suggest the estimating methods described above. Using them, you will know your numbers cold, release your three darts with confidence, and be able to fend off your inner underestimator. With each estimate, you will take a step toward building up the capital necessary to sustain your company and to invest for financial freedom.

Astute bidding likewise builds good long-term results. As mentioned at the outset of this chapter, bidding is not the same thing as estimating. Estimating is about figuring how much to charge for the on-site costs of building a project. Bidding comes in two phases, one before and one after estimating.

During the first phase, you are evaluating the project and determining whether you want to invest time in bidding for it. To summarize our earlier discussions of the subject: You are deciding if the project, client, and designer are a good fit for your company, whether the budget is adequate, and if your company and its trade partners have the skills to deliver the project competently.

You want to make damn sure the job provides you with a good chance of getting paid for your work and making a fair profit for your company. Yes, now and then, in order to help someone in need, to rescue an historical structure, or to keep a crew employed, you may go after a job on which you will not make a dime of pay for yourself or a profit for your company. If you want to get to financial independence, you will not do that often.

The second phase of bidding comes when estimating is complete. It involves the calculation of two crucial charges that must be included in your bid along with the charges for the construction itself. One is the charge for overhead – the expenses of running your company we have discussed previously. The other is the charge for profit.

If you've tuned in to the standard advice about charging for overhead and profit, you've likely been steered toward the use of fixed percentages. You may have been instructed to add 10 percent of construction costs for overhead and another 10 percent for profit. Alternately, you may have been advised to use the so-called "gross profit margin" (GPM) method. It, too, relies on use of a percentage, embedding it in a complex formula to produce "gross profit margin" – an odd term which means profit and overhead combined and expressed as a percentage of the total price for a job.

In the remodeling world, 40 percent gross profit margins are often encouraged by various industry experts as the "correct" fixed percentage and the one you should use for all your projects regardless of size, complexity, and other factors. That means that for every ten dollars clients pay, four dollars is for overhead and profit (4 ÷ 10 = 40 percent) and six dollars for the actual construction.

Both of the fixed percentage methods are inadequate for calculating overhead and profit. A better method involves adding overhead and profit in two separate steps, and flexibly, without reliance on fixed percentages. As we will discuss in detail below, the separation is necessary because overhead and profit are two very different creatures. Flexible use of percentages is necessary because of the financial realities.

Overhead is a set of expenses you must pay each month. With overhead your goal is to recapture, job by job, the expenses that each job imposes on your company. Use of a rigid percentage will not accomplish that. Why? Because in percentage terms, as we will see, different kinds of jobs impose very different overhead loads.

As for profit, it's an opportunity that fluctuates as the economy and demand for construction rises and falls. At times, you can mark up generously for profit. At other times, only meager profit is possible. Use of a rigid percentage does not match up with the realities of the marketplace.

I call the better method the capacity/time method. It enables you to appropriately allocate overhead to each of your projects. It puts you in the driver's seat and sets you up to make sound judgement calls about profit charges.

Using the capacity/time method, you first figure overhead on the basis of two factors: 1) *time*, namely how long a project that you are bidding on is projected to last; 2) *your capacity*, namely the number of projects you are capable of doing simultaneously.

To illustrate with a simple example: Assume you have three reliable project leads, each of whom can handle one project at a time. In that case, your capacity is three jobs at a time. Assume, also, that your overhead is $18,000 a month (including your pay for running your company).

In that case, your overhead per lead and project is $6,000 a month (18,000 ÷ 3 = 6,000). For a one-month repair job, your overhead charge needs to be $6,000. If you contract for a large addition that will take four months, your overhead charge needs to be $6,000 a month and a total for the four months of $24,000 (4 × 6,000 = 24,000).

That in a nutshell is how you use the capacity/time method to figure overhead. But why, you might be wondering, would you use it, other than for the general reasons mentioned a few paragraphs earlier?

The answer is this: The capacity/time method does away with a problem inherent in both of the fixed percentage methods. The problem arises from the fact that while repair work requires relatively high percentages of the total bid price for overhead, remodels require midrange percentages and custom home projects do fine with relatively low percentages. When construction company owners settle on a single percentage and use it across the board for very different size jobs, they may undercharge on small jobs and lose money. Or they may overcharge on big jobs and find themselves unable to compete.

As the example we will get to in a few paragraphs will demonstrate, the capacity/time method eliminates that potential miscarriage. It appropriately allocates overhead. For repair work and small remodels, it allocates a relatively high percentage of project cost for overhead. For larger projects, it allocates a relatively smaller percentage.

That is as it should be. Why? Because both small jobs and large jobs require a lead. Therefore, they use roughly equal proportions of your capacity and your overhead for each month that they are under construction. However, the small job will likely not involve costs for material and trade partners nearly as high per month as the big job. Therefore, overhead is a much higher proportion of total costs on the small job than on the big job.

Let's go to our example:

For the repair job that lasts one month, your construction costs are only for your lead, a helper, and a modest amount of material. No subs or costly materials such as cabinets are involved. So, let's say that costs run $24,000 for labor and $8,000 for material, for a total of $32,000 in direct costs of construction.

During the same month, the larger project involving the addition requires a lead plus a skilled carpenter and an apprentice, several trade partners, plus costly materials. Costs run $48,000 for labor, $20,000 for material, and $24,000 for trade partners, for a total of $92,000 in direct costs.

Both jobs, over the course of a month, use one-third of your capacity since both require a lead on the job full time. Therefore, they are both using about one-third of your overhead. Because the large job requires so much more expenditure for labor and material and subs, your overhead on that job is much smaller in proportion to direct costs of construction than for the smaller job.

Take a look at the numbers:

If your overhead is $6,000 a month per lead and project, then for the repair job overhead will be 19 percent of the labor and material costs (6,000 ÷ 32,000 = 19 percent). For the large job, overhead will be 6 percent of the labor, material and sub costs (6,000 ÷ 92,000 = 6 percent).

You will, of course add profit to your direct costs and your overhead when you package up your bid price for your client. Profit, too, can be charged on the basis of capacity and time. Ask yourself, how much profit do I need/want to realize per week with each of my crews? Bear in mind that smaller jobs use about as much of your capacity as bigger ones. Therefore, just as with overhead, you must charge profit on the smaller jobs that is a much higher percentage of direct costs than on larger jobs. At least you must do that if you want to earn enough profit to sustain your company and work toward financial freedom.

It might be, to take our example one final step forward, that you aim to earn a minimum of $4,000 profit a month on each of your projects. Therefore, on the one-month repair job you would be charging $24,000 for labor, $8,000 for material, $6,000 for overhead, and $4,000 for profit. With those four charges added up you would come to a $42,000 bid price to your clients

On the larger job, with the $4,000 monthly profit added to the labor, material, and trade partner costs, plus the overhead expenses, you would arrive at a total charge of $96,000 for each month the job was projected to run. For the full four months you estimated it would take, your charge would then be $384,000.

You might, however, feel the larger job saddled you with greater risks than the smaller job. Or you might see that construction services are, for the moment, in high demand. The marketplace will allow higher profits than in the two-year recession you just went through, during which survival, much less making a profit, was barely possible. You want to recover from the pounding you took during those years.

With those factors in mind you might decide to bump up your base profit charge. You might push it up from $4,000 to $6,000 or even much higher for certain large jobs or those including very costly materials and, therefore, added risk. Such judgment calls are an essential component of determining profit charges. At least they are essential if you are not content to establish them with a robotic application of a fixed percentage, which can lead to serious errors.

A final note: In order to introduce the idea of capacity/time allocation of overhead and profit, I have used straightforward examples here. I don't mean by that to suggest that use of the capacity/time method is without its own challenges. Appropriately allocating overhead and profit to a line of products is not easy in any industry (that's a broader topic for another day). It can't be reduced to simplicity even in construction.

One challenge you face with capacity/time is adjusting markup when you are not operating at your usual capacity and have fewer jobs in your pipeline than you are capable of handling – as may well happen during a recession. In that case, you'd have three choices: Increase markup on the jobs you do have; cover your overhead but back off on profit so that your price to a client remains competitive;

or draw on your capital reserves to cover part of your overhead until you can get back up to speed. Each such choice will involve thinking and judgment calls.

You may have to revise the capacity/time method if you run a design/build firm. Here perhaps the best solution is to separate design and construction into two separate entities for bidding and accounting purposes. Use capacity/time to allocate overhead and profit to your construction side. Use another method for the design side, perhaps by charging on an hourly basis, with overhead and profit incorporated into your hourly rate.

You may have to adjust if your projects are run by project managers who may be running one very large project or several small ones. In that case, your capacity is determined by your number of project managers rather than by your number of lead carpenters. You will have to determine how much overhead and profit to assign to each of a PM's projects. That may be particularly tricky when a project manager is running several projects simultaneously, with each project expected to span a different period of time.

Capacity/time is definitely not without its own challenges. It does retain its advantage. It positions you to recapture overhead expenses and earn profit on the basis of your considered judgment. You aren't merely off-loading responsibility to some arbitrary industry formula. To borrow terms from Michael Anschel, owner of a design/build firm in Minneapolis, the capacity/time method is "dynamic" rather than "passive."

The numbers I used above to illustrate the capacity/time method are hypothetical. You might be wondering just how much you actually should charge. My best answer: For overhead, charge enough to fully recapture your tightly managed expenses for each project, whether large or small. For profit, as a rule of thumb, charge whatever profit the market and your ethics will allow. Remember, making profit over the long term is difficult in construction. But make it you must in order to build up capital reserves for the hard times, provide your employees with profit sharing during good times, and build up capital for investment. Make it when you can.

As we have discussed earlier, actual profit margins – "realized" profits to use the technical term – are, on average, low in our industry. Construction pros do, however, often aim for much higher than average profits – anywhere from 10 percent to 25 percent of their total revenue and even more. During good times in some situations, such as booming metro areas, some pros actually achieve those profits.

With estimating and bidding complete and construction underway, you arrive at another crucial numbers task: accounting. To return to the metaphor used in the chapter "Your Right Stuff," you need to track the *flow* of money into and out of your company. You need to see exactly where it is flowing from and where it is flowing to. Here we will survey the flows that must be watched most carefully.

To begin with, you want to keep an eye on how the outflow of money for a job, the costs of constructing it, are stacking up against your estimated costs. Did framing lumber cost you an amount close to the estimated amount? How did your actual payouts for framing labor compare to your projections? Ditto for every other division of work in the project.

Tracking costs on your jobs will enable you to see whether or not an estimate is off. If it is running off, you will see where you are in error. With that knowledge, you will know where you must develop your estimating data and sharpen procedures for future estimates.

When a project ends, or in the case of a large project, periodically during construction, you want to look at its profitability, or lack thereof. Is more money flowing into the project than is flowing out from it? In other words, are you making or losing money on the project? If you are making money, is the amount reasonably close to what you had intended to earn? If you are running low, are there adjustments you can make without compromising quality?

You also want to keep an eye on profitability for your company as a whole (or mounting losses if you've hit a bad patch) as each year progresses. As we have emphasized earlier, when you figure profitability make sure to account for the fact that the pay you take for yourself is not profit. It's an overhead expense. You have to deduct it from your company's income, along with all other costs, to determine profitability.

If you are not making a profit after taking reasonable pay for yourself, consider that a warning sign.

In addition to monitoring profitability on each job and for your company as a whole, you should track the variations in the amount of profit your company is earning from one year to the next. If you are growing volume but not profit, you will want to ask yourself, Is the growth worthwhile? Is it smart?

The greater your volume, the greater your chances of getting hit with those pernicious profit costs. If your volume is steadily increasing but your profits are not going up commensurately, you are increasing exposure without increasing protection. You are expanding risk without strengthening the buffer necessary to handle the possible consequences. That's like loading up a truck beyond the carrying capacity of its springs, shock absorbers, and brakes, then heading down a steep hill on a road filled with potholes.

You must also monitor your cash position, both currently and as it is likely to develop going forward. It's easy enough to know your current cash position. It's the amount of money you have in your business bank account. But as a builder you also need to be able to project what your cash position will be in a week, a month, or even further along in the calendar. After all, if profit is the shock absorber for your construction business, then cash is its fuel. You need to make sure you have enough in the tank to complete the trip.

Doing that is straightforward enough. You first figure how much you are owed and when payments will be flowing into your company. Then you figure how much you owe to others and when your payments to them will be flowing out. Start with your current cash position (the money you have in your business account), add the money due to flow in, subtract the money that will be going out, and you've projected a future cash position.

To project your cash situation even further out, figure income that is not yet earned and expenses not yet incurred on projects that are underway. Don't, however, stray into the wishful thinking of counting on positive cash flow from projects you have not even started, much less those you have not yet signed a contract for. Construction pros have been known to fall prey to that temptation.

If the amount that will be going out will exceed the amount that will be flowing in, you may be heading for trouble. Against that trouble, construction accountants sometimes advise establishing a line of credit. That's a promise by a bank to extend a loan to you when you need it.

I say, okay, if you absolutely have to set up a line of credit, go for it. But I urge differently: Operate frugally. Build up ample capital reserves. Then you will never have trouble paying your bills. You will save interest charges on loans.

Banks don't "give" loans, though we often say they do. They issue loans in order to earn profits of their own. When you take a loan, you are agreeing to share your potential profits with the bank. Better that you keep your earnings for yourself. Much better if your purpose is to get to financial independence.

To ensure financial success, take command of the money flow. Don't let it just happen. Don't wait for money to flow in. Make sure it flows in promptly. As the old construction adage advises: Bill early, as soon as you have earned payment by completing work or incurring other costs, like deposits for windows, on the client's behalf. Bill often. Collect immediately. Including for change orders.

Likewise monitor the outgoing flow. Make sure that only legitimate bills are being paid. Be certain that no trade partner is accidentally (or deliberately) double billing you. If you employ a bookkeeper, establish a system to ensure they are not diverting any of your money flow into their accounts. Embezzlement happens. Often it is committed by a long-term, trusted employee.

If you are experiencing callbacks, track their causes so that you can eliminate them. Left unchecked, callback costs can accelerate. One builder told me that when he stepped back from direct management of the company he had founded, his accounting system alerted him to a 500 percent increase in the amount of money surging out of his company to cover callbacks.

To manage overhead effectively, you want to see your expenses broken down. For example, you don't want to lump all office expenses together. You want to know how much is going out for rent, how much for computers and software, how much is steadily trickling out for phones, bookkeeping, stamps, paper, ink, and utilities. Then you can zero in on areas of excess outflow and figure out how to stem it.

As I have stressed so often, especially in "Lean and Frugal," you must monitor and regularly pare away overhead costs and shut off time leaks.

You may also wish to monitor what these days is described as "the sales funnel." How many leads are coming in each month? Where are they coming from? From references? Or as a result of that new marketing campaign you invested in? Which leads actually lead to profitable jobs?

Ask yourself: Given what I see in the sales funnel, is it worth investing more in the marketing campaign? Or should I double down on taking care of and staying in touch with my existing customers? Or both?

If you are new to the construction business, the challenge of keeping track of your money flows and handling all the accounting tasks may feel overwhelming. Please don't be intimidated. You don't need a business degree, though a few good junior college courses might help. With study, you can learn to handle accounting – as I did, starting with so little financial education beforehand I did not know how to balance a checkbook. With low-cost software you can handle accounting efficiently and effectively.

Using the software, you need only input the payments you make and the payments you receive. Once you have properly set it up, perhaps with guidance from a consultant deeply knowledgeable about construction accounting, your software will then create what are variously termed "reports" or "statements." They inform you about all your key money flows. Accountants, naturally, have their own special terms for the various kinds of reports and statements.

"Job costing" reports will tell you how job costs are running as compared to your estimates. "Profit and loss (P&L)" statements will keep you informed of profit (or, heaven forbid, loss) by job and by the month or the year to date.

Another report will tally up "receivables" (payments you are due) and "payables" (money you owe) to project a future cash position.

Your software will also provide you with a statement called a "balance sheet." It will display the value of what you own, your assets, alongside what you owe, your debts. By subtracting debts from assets, it gives you your "net worth."

Balance sheet net worth can, as explained earlier in "Thought Remodeling," be misleading if you take "net worth" too literally and equate it with the actual value of your company. A lean and well-run construction company may have very little in assets other than a truck or two, some tools and equipment, and adequate capital reserves. If so, a balance sheet would indicate that it has modest net worth. But it may be quite valuable. Its value derives from its relationships with its clients, crew, and trade partners – and its excellent estimating, bidding, and accounting procedures.

Those relationships and procedures result in earning power. Good bidding and estimating lead to profitable contracts with reliable clients. The crew and trade partners build durable and good-looking projects efficiently. The happy clients refer new customers. Good money is made on one project after another.

A balance sheet does not include in its net worth figure the relationships and procedures and the financial results they enable. It may, therefore, grossly understate the real value of a construction operation. One lean company, whose owner is now retired, had (in 2021 dollars) only about $25,000 worth of equipment plus an ample capital reserve on its balance sheet. But during good years, it earned, in owner's pay and profit, close to three-quarters of a million dollars a year. That was a valuable operation even if its balance sheet did not report much "net worth."

There in a nutshell are the essentials of construction accounting: Job costing. P&L. Receivables, payables, and cash position. Monitoring overhead, callbacks, and the sales funnel. Balance sheet.

Do you want to steadily travel the road to financial independence? Please build good estimating, bidding, and accounting practices into your company. Do the necessary hard work. *You must know your numbers.*

Beyond estimating, bidding, and accounting lies a different sort of financial task: cash management. But before getting to it we must turn our attention to another matter. That's protecting your profit to ensure that you actually will have cash to manage and to invest.

Protecting Your Profit

You will effectively protect your profit with the kinds of practices we have discussed in earlier chapters: Investing in your people. Running a lean operation. Trimming away wasted motion. Building to high quality standards.

Beyond these practices, there are specific protections that construction pros can place around their businesses. Think of them as a series of concentric rings or barricades that prevent assaults on the company.

The outermost ring is choosing the right customers. You don't want to let a bad customer into your operations. One attorney warns, "With the bad customer, no contract, no matter how good, will help. The bad customer is going to sue anyhow."

Even if they do not sue, bad customers can sap your energy and disrupt your focus. They connive and manipulate in attempts to get more for less. They distract you and your people from getting on with the job. They make constant demands on your time, as did a client of one custom home builder. She climbed up ladders to inspect the nail pattern in the framing. She worried at the crew about the accuracy of their cuts. She demanded constant meetings with the builder so she could quiz and advise him about his procedures, though she knew little about construction.

A bad client may refuse to pay. "Have your lawyer call my lawyer," a client told a friend of mine after declining to pay him the final $100,000 on a million-dollar job. The builder did not call his lawyer. He preferred to let the client stiff him. He did not want to lie awake at night for years thinking about a lawsuit, bleeding money for attorney's fees.

Max, as you will see in a few pages, was doing well overall as he reached the midpoint of his career. He was not, however, good at avoiding bad customers. He did not choose his customers carefully. Pridefully, he said that he could work with anyone. He claimed that working with difficult clients strengthened his ability to be patient while holding his ground.

Three times he signed contracts for year-long jobs with bad customers. One was a crook who was fired for embezzling funds from the nonprofit she had founded. The other two were wealthy bullies with a huge sense of entitlement and the habit of throwing tantrums when they did not get their way.

Partway through each of the three projects, Max had angry run-ins with the clients. He threatened the embezzler with foreclosure on her home when she tried to withhold a payment. She paid. To one of the bullies he said, "I don't know if you are threatening me physically or with legal action, but I promise you that you will lose badly either way." The man hesitated, looked down at the floor, and apologized. Max put down the other bully as well.

For a time, Max felt proud of his victories. But eventually he realized he had been lucky. Each of the situations could have led to years of energy-sapping legal entanglement. He would have been better off avoiding the clients in the first place.

Avoiding bad clients is easier said than done. I do not know of a way to quickly determine whether a potential client is likely to be a good person to sign a contract with or not. In fact, in my experience, first impressions are often wrong. As a friend of mine who runs a large business says, "First interviews are where two people get together and lie to one another."

That's especially a problem if you do "free" competitive bidding. Then you usually get a chance for only a first impression before going to contract. The next time you see the client is likely to be after they have accepted your bid. You need more interaction than that to size them up. Competitive bidding does not offer it, another reason for moving beyond bidding and estimating for free, as we discussed in "Constructing Profit Opportunities."

When you move up to charging for preconstruction services, you will have multiple meetings with the client. As you see them grappling with the real costs and challenges of their project, you have an improved chance to take their measure. If you hear warning bells – quickness to anger, lack of patience, blaming, or self-centeredness – you can withdraw from the relationship.

Even before much interaction takes place, you increase protection by contracting to provide preconstruction services for a fee rather than bidding for free. It automatically sorts the better from the potentially damaging clients. People who want to exploit you for free estimating are, by definition, dubious clients. People who understand that it is fair to compensate you for the valuable work of estimating and other preconstruction services are better prospects.

Good insurance, both liability and workers' compensation, provides a second ring of protection. Liability insurance is overwhelmingly complicated. To begin with, it is a constantly moving target. Policies are always in flux. One year they offer coverages for one mix of building failures and the next year for a somewhat different mix. To make the waters muddier, different types of policies offer different coverages.

The policies are written in prose so dense and legalistic that deciphering it is like learning a foreign language, say ancient Greek. The different companies offering those opaque policies have very different records of actually paying up when claims are made against the holder of the policy, i.e., you and your company (or me and mine).

Keeping up with the constant changes and variations, never mind trying to make out what the policies actually promise and withhold while evaluating the companies that sell them, is a full-time job. It's a rare construction pro who would have the inclination or time to take it on.

You have to select the right person to do the job for you. That's not the good-natured agent down the street who offers car and home insurance. It's certainly not some other construction pro, including me – which is why I will limit myself to giving you only a broad overview of the process of selecting a policy and, hopefully, a nudge in a productive direction.

You need an expert. You need to locate a reliable insurance broker, *one who specializes in construction insurance*, to manage policy selection for you. Construction insurance is like everyday auto and homeowner's insurance in that it protects you and your assets. But it's more complicated and very different at the level of the particulars. That's why you need a specialist. Likely you want the go-to guy for well-established construction companies in your area.

If they are in fact good, they will guide you to a choice of a suitable policy, acquainting you with prime considerations in the process. They will compare several policies that might be good choices. They'll explain the pros and cons of each.

They will offer you policies from companies that meet several criteria: The companies will have a respectable overall financial rating. They will actually cover the costs if you are hit with a serious claim. They will not have conduct issues with local regulators or excessive poor reviews from customers.

They will make sure that the policies do not exclude from coverage any of the types of work you take on. Construction pros have paid fat premiums for years on end only to be told, when they do have a claim, that it arose from work their policy did not cover. Treacy Duerfeldt, founder of a nationwide alliance of insurance agents that serve the construction industry, says he has seen policies for swimming pool builders that *excluded excavation from coverage*. Good grief! Now do you see why you need a broker expert in construction insurance?

Your broker will explain to you the difference between policies which fully cover claims against you for work done years back, not just a current year, and those which may leave you holding the bag for past work. They will also compare costs of different policies for you. At the same time, they will warn you to be wary of low bidders, just as you might caution your clients to be wary of low bidders for construction work. "As in everything," says Duerfeldt, "you get what you pay for." Or as I like to say, "Cheap often isn't."

That applies in spades to the second component of your insurance protections – workers' compensation insurance. Our employees do dangerous work. We have an obligation to provide for them in case of injury. Because the comp coverage is so costly, it can be tempting to skimp on it. If we do, we put ourselves at risk along with our workers, even when the laws in our state don't require workers' comp.

A prominent high-end residential construction company in my area went for a cheapo comp provider. One of their workers was disabled in a jobsite accident. The lowball provider either could not or would not cover the worker's claim. His lawyers went after the construction company. The settlement the lawyers won put the company out of business.

I could tell you other such cautionary tales. Hopefully you don't need to hear them. I also have experienced insurance companies who pay fair claims promptly and without dispute. A workers' comp policy from a financially sound, reliable, and reputable insurance company is a must. It will protect you and your assets.

As a third ring of protection, a construction company can incorporate. The degrees of protection provided by incorporation vary from state to state. The essential protection is this: If your company is sued, your personal assets, including your investments, will not be as likely to be on the table.

You can put your construction company and your other assets inside different corporations – the company in one, each of several rental properties in another, and so on. Then, if someone brings a claim against your company, they will have to "pierce the veil" provided by incorporation should they try to go after your assets. Likewise, if a tenant in one rental brings a claim, they will be constrained from targeting your company's capital reserves or other properties.

In "Resources," you will find a listing for a book that will walk you through the basics of incorporation – particularly of limited liability corporations (LLCs). They are the simplest of the several types of corporations. Typically, they are the alternative chosen by construction pros.

A fourth ring of protection is perhaps the most valuable of all. It will give you the knowledge you need to successfully set up the aforementioned protections. It is less obvious than the protections covered so far. In fact, it might seem to you that it would weaken your position rather than strengthening and protecting it. The fourth ring is sharing knowledge with your peers, especially with other construction pros *in your area*.

That does go against the grain. Even though we will learn from them in turn, we instinctively are afraid of sharing ideas with our potential competitors. We shouldn't be. By strengthening them, we strengthen ourselves. We improve our position in our markets. We are much better off competing against capable pros than against guys still stumbling around in the dark and underbidding projects.

As I look back on my own career, I can see that the best move I ever made was joining a group of my competitors that met regularly to talk about the construction business. There I met my mentors. There I was guided to a good insurance broker.

There I learned what to include in my contracts both for preconstruction and for construction work, such as a comprehensive change order procedure; a requirement for frequent and prompt payments;

a clear statement that the client must communicate about the project only with the lead or with myself, not with other crew or trade partners; even a limit on the amount of time I and my leads were required to talk with a client each week.

There, at the meetings of my builders' group and in conversation with the friends I made there, I was schooled not only in the principles of company management but also in details of construction technology – like flashing and other water management details.

A particularly crucial protection that my group alerted me to is the need for a construction company to grow, if at all, with prudence and preparation. Many members of the group chose to run compact companies with just one or two crews and minimal office help. Others created sizable businesses with fifty or more employees and gross revenues (in 2021 dollars) of $20 million a year and up.

The larger companies that survived accomplished their growth a step at a time, preparing for more growth before they took it on, and over many years. Their owners are understandably proud of what they have accomplished. They are also candid in admitting that they have come close to financial collapse at times. As Paul Eldrenkamp pointed out (see "Thought Remodeling"), growth is hazardous in construction – not impossible, just seriously hazardous.

My builders' group called itself the Splinter Group. It was informally organized, refreshingly free of bureaucracy and costs. An article I published about it is available at *JLC* online. Perhaps the article will inspire you to start your own group. The article does suggest first steps. They may well could turn out to be the most productive steps you ever take to strengthen and protect your business. With the exception of two individuals who took advantage of what they learned in the Splinter Group to get one-up on other members, none of its several dozen long-term members failed in business. That's evidence that poetic justice exists. It's also a remarkable record and evidence that sharing with your peers can strengthen your own construction operation.

As Max progressed, he built his company around principles like those we have looked at so far in this book. He teamed with his employees and trade partners to get work done correctly at his jobs. He communicated fully and clearly with clients, sometimes to a fault it seems. A client who hired him for multiple jobs sometimes chided him, "You already crossed that *t* and dotted that *i*, Max. Let's move on."

To himself he would admit, "I am thorough. Maybe I overdo it sometimes. But for a builder that's a good thing." Building, Max rationalized, was not the right career for people whose priority was a laid-back life or for whom "good enough" was adequate. The liabilities were too great. Max preferred to err in the direction of protecting his profits too much rather than not enough.

Max and his crew and trade partners bore down on the details. One of their customers praised their work as "bulletproof." Max just shrugged and said to the crew, "Yeah. What's the point otherwise?" They agreed.

They did make mistakes and ran into unanticipated problems. When they did, Max let their customers know about both the problems and their solutions. The meticulousness and the candor inspired trust and loyalty in his customers and caused them to refer their friends to Max. He and his crews always had work and their projects steadily grew in size, complexity, and challenge.

As his company matured, Max realized he needed sources of information and guidance. He began reading industry journals. He joined a local association of builders sponsored by a national construction organization.

Max noticed that members of the group had emphatically different opinions about certain issues, like marketing. Max adopted the thinking of those who favored letting their work do the talking. He leaned away from those who stressed the cultivation of a "professional image." To Max it looked like the image was made up of nothing more than fancy jobsite signs and conference rooms intended to impress clients. It seemed to Max to have nothing to do with adherence to actual professional standards of ethics or performance.

Max favored the lean practices that enabled him to hold down his prices to clients while still earning good pay and profits. He would not have argued that was "professional," but he thought it was ethical.

When he needed more of an office than simply a desk in the corner of his home, he resisted renting or buying space. He designed a simple, shed-roofed structure and built it in his backyard with material salvaged from his projects.

He paid his people top dollar, granted them autonomy and treated them with respect. That enabled him to attract and hold top-notch leads, carpenters, and trade partners. They were so good Max needed no costly layers of project managers between the leads and himself. He told his builders' group that he had concluded that three great leads produced better work than three so-so leads who needed an expensive project manager supervising them. And they did it for less cost.

Max also went without office staff. He let his voice mail take phone calls. He simplified accounting down to necessities and contracted out his bookkeeping, calling on his accountant only for end-of-year tax returns,

Estimating he did himself, building a powerful spreadsheet and a set of labor productivity records that enabled him to do it rapidly and accurately. He did not have to do much of it. At his builders' group, Max had learned about the movement away from bidding for free. He became an adherent, signing contracts with customers to provide preconstruction services for a fee and with the understanding that he would not only collaborate with the client and designer to plan the job but would also build it.

As a result, he produced estimates only for those jobs he was all but sure to build – for though there was always a possibility a client could decide to move to another builder or to not build at all, that happened rarely. Gone were the days of producing endless "free" bids which very often did not lead to construction work. As Max's jobs increased in size, he found himself having to produce estimates only half a dozen times a year – and he was compensated at professional rates for that work.

Max did all he could to reduce complexity in his operation and winnowed out everything that he could do without. "I want as few moving parts as possible," he said. "Then not much can go wrong. What does go wrong is easy to fix." Because not much did go wrong, profit was protected. It stayed in Max's or the company's accounts rather than going out for profit costs.

Max often wondered why many of his fellow builders insisted on creating such elaborate operations, top-heavy with office staff. Did they not see that they were burdening, not strengthening, their businesses; building not fortresses, but financial sieves; threatening, not protecting, profitability?

As best he could make out it was because they believed that their elaborate platforms were necessary to achieve growth in volume, that growth was the path to profitability, and that greater profits gave rise to greater self-esteem.

Max became steadily more dubious about the formulation. He regularly met construction pros who said they had tried for volume, and then, when that did not work, tried for yet more volume, only to discover that the more volume they achieved the less money they made. Max's heavy equipment trade partner told him, "I used to have twenty guys running my rigs. Now I'm back to four. I am making a lot more than I did with twenty people. And I'm having a hell of a lot more fun."

Max noticed that he sometimes did feel the allure of an ever bigger, glossier operation. He found himself wondering if happiness, that sense of being the "man about town" that Oliver had once spoken of when he was rapidly increasing his volume, did lie in the direction of rapid growth. But Max always decided that, for himself at least, the answer was no. He'd let his company grow organically, steadily, and not too fast – if at all.

What might too fast look like, Max wondered? He found his

answer in a book by Thomas Schleifer (whose concise, expensive, well-worth-every-cent book is also listed in "Resources"). The answer was: 1) Never take on a job that is more than twice the size of any you have handled before, and 2) Don't take on an annual volume of work that is more than twice your company's previously greatest annual volume. To Schleifer's two warnings, Max added a third of his own: If you do sharply increase year-over-year volume, don't increase it again until you are certain that your systems and personnel are ready for it.

Max rejected industry pundits who advised, "If you are not growing, you are dying" – and by "growing" made clear they meant rapidly growing volume. Max concluded that was nonsense. Were you dying if you were happy running a compact company that did great work, provided good jobs to people you cared about, made good money. and sustained itself?

Max came across an article that resonated with his own thinking. It was about Fritz Maytag, the founder of Anchor Brewery. "We thought we had to grow," Maytag said. "It occurred to me that you could have a small prestigious business. Just because it is the best around does not mean you have to expand."

Max felt very fortunate. Starting with almost no knowledge of business, he had somehow built a sturdy construction company. With its committed crews, lean business systems, supportive clients, and organic growth, it demanded less and less of Max's time. He was able to begin to explore investing and saw that financial freedom was in reach.

At exactly that point, Max proceeded to put all he had accomplished in jeopardy. He violated every cautionary rule about growth he'd embraced. He took on four large jobs simultaneously. Two were more than twice the size of the biggest projects he had previously handled. The total dollar value of the four was more than double any volume he had taken on previously. All of them were complex and several featured difficult access.

As construction proceeded, profit costs struck. At one project, work stopped for weeks as trees and power lines taken down by a storm were cleared from the road leading to the jobsite. Meanwhile overhead expenses had to be paid and the crew employed at small jobs Max gathered up.

At another project the crew was repeatedly slowed as the architect stalled on requests for information because he had underpriced his services and was bleeding cash on the project.

At a third, which involved the construction of a residential addition on a steep lot, a storm rolled in on New Year's Eve. Rain pounded the work site, flattening plants, blotting out vision of nearby hills, churning up mud and spreading it across the site. The downpour steadily eroded a ten-foot-high cut Max's excavator had made in the hillside. The eroding cut edged closer and closer to the foundation supporting the client's big garage.

Max got on the phone. He asked his crew to come to the jobsite. He called trade partners: His drill rig operator. The guy with the big front-end loader. His concrete pumper. A gravel pumper. His concrete and steel and heavy lumber suppliers.

Well, it was New Year's Eve, they said, but okay, this was an emergency. Max had always done right by them. They'd head right over with the needed material and equipment.

With his crew and equipment operators, Max went to work in the storm to save the garage. Laboring in mud up to their ankles, the crew teamed with the drill operator to plunge deep holes along the edge of the cut. Eight times the front-end loader skidded down the hillside with a steel H-beam strapped to the bucket and executed a four-wheel slide into the work area. The crew unstrapped each beam from the bucket and chained it to the drill rig's arm. The rig operator lifted the beam and dropped it into a freshly drilled hole. Max and his crew held each piece of steel plumb, grappled with the mud-slimy hose from the concrete pump, slid it into the hole, and filled the hole.

The weight of the steel repeatedly forced the drill rig's treads down into the mud. The rig tilted sideways, threatening to topple over. Max and the crew dragged sheets of ¾ inch subflooring from their stock down the hill and dropped it alongside the drill rig. Pressing his bucket down through the mud, the rig operator levered his treads up onto the plywood. The rig stayed upright long enough for another piece of steel to be placed. Then more plywood had to be hauled through the mud and dropped into place and the drill rig again levered upright.

Using a trick he had learned during his years as a framing carpenter, Max spun 6x6 wood beams on his foot, rotating them under his circular saw. As cut lengths fell away, the crew heaved them into the slots in the steel uprights. Steadily they raised a retaining wall. With the wall built to full height, the crew dragged a hose down from the gravel pumper. and shot tons of drain rock into the void behind the wall The erosion was halted a few feet shy of the garage foundation.

Max and his crew, mud now coating their jeans and jackets, their faces and their hair, high-fived one another. Max screamed a joyous "Yes, we did it!" The garage was saved, along with the million-dollar supercar that, as Max later learned, was parked inside.

Eventually, Max got through the four projects. His employee centered practices paid off. His employees stayed with him, battling through the bad weather and the difficult access, and doing their usual clean work. The clients were appreciative, even admiring.

But there were costs as well. Max had often been exhausted and short-tempered, even with family, friends, and trade partners. He bruised relationships. Some never recovered.

"Why did I do that?" Max wondered. "Why did I do exactly what I knew not to do, what every wise voice was telling me to not do, what Oliver's experience with excessive growth taught me not to do?"

Max made himself face the answer. Vanity. Max had taken the projects during a recession. For years at their meetings, Max had heard his fellow builders brag about their volumes of work. Now there was a recession, and many were struggling. It was Max's chance to casually mention "Looks like we'll be doing about eight million this year," even as other builders were starved for work. Max basked in their envy and admiration.

Yes, vanity. The results retaught Max the lessons about growth and also the truth of another good business maxim, an ancient one: Pride goeth before a fall.

Max was lucky, far luckier than many construction pros who tread into arrogant growth. He did not go broke. Though he barely recovered his out-of-pocket overhead on the project involving the garage rescue, earning no pay for himself, the other jobs worked out financially. They provided for substantial profit sharing with the crew. Max felt especially good giving them their checks, thinking they had surely earned them during his year of overreaching. Those projects also provided Max with substantial profit that he stored away in his capital accounts.

Max intended to put his capital to work in investments. He saw that he faced a new challenge. He did not know how to invest other than by putting cash into certificates of deposit or treasury bills. That had been fine during earlier years when interest rates had risen to historical highs. But now rates were back to moderate levels. Max realized that he was going to have to seek out other possibilities. Just as he had learned how to run a construction company, he now had to learn how to operate as an investor.

PART THREE:
Building Financial Intelligence

- Managing Cash
- Investment Literacy I: Principles
- Investment Literacy II: Practices
- Deploying Capital
- Friction, Debt, Max, and Taxes

Managing Cash

I have attended hundreds of meetings of builders. If any single topic gets the most attention, it is profit. Curiously, I have never heard a presentation on what to do with profit in case you are fortunate enough to earn some and hold on to it. Nor have I heard one on managing cash as it flows through a construction company. Cash management and deployment of profit are the subjects we will turn to here in Part III.

Cash management and accounting are not the same thing. Accounting, as we have discussed, is about *tracking* the flow of money through your company so that you know where it is coming from and where it is going. Cash management is about *directing* the flow of money to the right places. Accounting is observation. Cash management is command and control.

Cash management is what the legendary grandmother does. Her family farm is making money. The cows are giving a lot of milk. The crops are abundant. Prices at the market are good. Cash is flowing in. The grandmother takes command of it. She sets up a series of envelopes in her steel box with a hasp and lock. One envelope is for next month's expenses, another for the winter's expenses, a third for the new tractor the family hopes to buy, others for charity, holidays, and good times. Another envelope is labeled "Rainy Day Fund" or maybe "Emergency Fund" or simply "Hard Times." The grandmother divides each week's income from the market into the envelopes. She's got control of the farm's cash.

These days when financial sophisticates talk about cash flow they speak, metaphorically, of "buckets" rather than referring to "envelopes." But underlying the new metaphor and grandmother's envelopes is the same idea. As money flows in, you apportion it among your array of "buckets," i.e., a set of accounts at financial institutions. Then the cash is where you need it when you need it.

As your company expands its volume of work and enjoys greater amounts of cash flow, you will gradually increase the number of buckets you use. When you are just starting out you may have just a single bucket. You are running a one-person company. You have a couple of suppliers and relationships with a framer, plumber, drywaller, and maybe a few other trade partners. Briefly, you can get by with just a checking account. You will put all the money you earn into that bucket and take cash out as you need it for both business and personal expenses.

But soon you will want to add additional buckets. Leaving the first bucket for owner's pay you draw from the company and personal expenses, you establish another bucket, a second checking account at a different bank. It will serve as the business account into which you can deposit income and from which you pay expenses.

When you pay yourself for the work you do for your company, you will write a check from the business account and deposit it into the personal account. That's in keeping with the principle we have emphasized earlier: Your pay is not company profit. When you pay yourself for the work you do for your company, your company is incurring an expense.

You would do well to set up a third bucket early in your career. That is a bucket for taxes. Paying taxes is an unavoidable aspect of running your own business. You may not like that. You may feel that government takes way too much of your hard-earned income and then proceeds to waste it.

If so, you may be tempted to evade paying taxes. Try it to any significant degree and there is a good chance you will get caught. The IRS is all over the construction industry. If you do get caught, you will have to pay not only the taxes but penalties, perhaps so heavy that will they compromise your financial future. Or worse. "If you decide to evade taxes," advises Gary Eldred, author of the book on real estate investing I strongly recommend in "Resources," "line up a competent property manager to look after your properties while you are in prison."

That is where you would belong. People who cheat on their taxes leave those of us who do not cheat to foot the bill for the infrastructure, law enforcement, national defense, educational institutions, environmental protection, medical research, and other services from which they and their families benefit. Lock 'em up!

With personal, business operations, and tax buckets in place, you must make sure there is always enough money in the buckets to pay your expenses. You will do that using the methods we discussed in the last chapter. You will project income and expenses – including tax obligations, which you can calculate together with your accountant – for the coming week, month, and longer, and determine whether income is going to exceed expenses or not.

If you see that you are going to be short of cash, your best response would be to tighten up on expenses, especially personal expenses and company overhead. Do without. Tighten your belt. Even if you are already practicing frugality, you may be able to trim back just enough without impairing your projects or office operations to get through the cash bottleneck.

If worse comes to worst, you may have to seek a loan from family or a friend. Or perhaps you can ask trade partners and suppliers you have paid promptly for years if they would be willing to wait for payment. Alternately, you can, as mentioned earlier, go to a bank and open up a line of credit.

If you seek financial freedom, doing without for a time is much better than borrowing money. As we have noted, debtors share their future earnings with their lender in the form of interest payments. Better that you preserve those earnings for your company and yourself.

Hopefully, rather than coming up short, you are easily topping up all three of your buckets. Now you may face an interior challenge – an inner overspender, the sibling rival of Paul Eldrenkamp's inner underestimator that we met in "Numbers."

Judith Miller, a construction industry financial strategist, cautions against the inner overspender. She reports that she has, "over the years, seen many companies fall prey to the arrogance of profitability." Business is booming and they are on a roll, but they fritter away their cash on overly ambitious speculative projects and big boys' toys. "They do that without a sufficient understanding of how they are impacting their cash flow and development of a sufficient war chest of money for protection in bad times."

Perhaps you are conservative with cash, governed by an inner frugalista, rather than an inner overspender. Then you will have an edge when it comes to creating and filling your next bucket. It's the equivalent of the grandmother's "Rainy Day" envelope. It's the "war chest for bad times" Miller describes. Technically, it's termed a "capital reserves account."

You should set up and begin to fill the capital reserves bucket as soon as you are able. It is needed even by a company that is very small and in its start-up years.

Rainy days and bad times come in construction. They come to all of us, no matter how knowledgeable, no matter how well-organized and well-prepared, no matter the size and maturity of our businesses. They come in the form of recessions and all the other profit costs listed in the "Tools" section at the back of this book. We must have cash in reserve to handle them.

You may be wondering, Where should I keep my capital reserves? To keep things simple, you may initially want to keep the reserves in a separate account at the same bank where you have your checking account for business operations. With the buckets side by side at a single institution, you can easily transfer funds from the reserves to the operations bucket, and vice versa, as necessary. As your company grows, and the reserves grow with it, you may want to move them to an institution where they can reap greater yields than the checking account interest your bank offers.

You may also be asking, "Just how much should I have in that capital reserves bucket?" Different construction industry experts have different opinions. Victoria Downing, the head of Remodelers Advantage, a respected provider of peer group-based education and consulting services, suggests having enough cash in reserve to cover four to six months of overhead, including owner's pay.

A construction company can, however, endure stretches much longer than half a year during which it cannot earn enough to cover its out-of-pocket overhead expenses and also pay its owner (never mind earn a profit). My own sense is that a company should have at least a year's worth of overhead including owner's pay, or 10 percent of peak annual revenue, in reserve.

Yes, that means when you reach a half million a year in sales, you should have $50,000 in reserve; at $1 million, $100,000; and so on. Those figures are merely intuitive on my part. I realize they may seem excessive. But several construction pros, from one with a small remodeling company to another with annual revenues over $10 million, have acknowledged the value of the guideline. They kept that 10 percent of revenue in reserve, and it got them through difficult years they might not otherwise have survived.

Even well-established companies can scrape the bottom of an inadequate reserves bucket during recessions. The consequences can be severe. Desperate for cash, you bid dangerously low. You pressure your customers for faster payment. You stall on payments to your trade partners and suppliers. You can't make payroll and have to ask your employees to wait for their checks. A project lead is embarrassed when their favorite clerk at the lumberyard tells them, "Sorry, we can't sell to you. Your company hasn't been paying its bills." For lack of cash reserves, you are damaging the trusting relationships you have built up over the years.

In a couple of years, with healthy profits, a construction company can build up reserves to 10 percent of revenue, whether it's a few hundreds of thousands or several million dollars annually. It takes effort. You have to throttle the inner overspender. You have to hold your pay down to the level you need to maintain a healthy lifestyle and not more.

Companies that do build reserves are positioned to get through hard times. They can emerge with their reputations intact. They have a much better chance of being among the construction companies that survive and never crash but, instead, prosper.

If you do run through your cash reserves, you have to build them up again. With that done, you have a bucket for business operating expenses, another for personal expenses, a third for taxes, and a fourth filled to the brim with cash for hard times. You have created a financially strong construction company.

Now the fun begins. Your company is earning more than it needs to pay its bills, protect itself, and support you and your family. It has surplus cash flow. You could take the extra cash, put it in your personal bucket, and splurge. However, as a reader attracted to this book, you are likely more inclined toward achieving financial freedom than going on a luxury cruise. You will set up a fifth bucket. That is your bucket for investment capital.

To use the capital effectively you will need to ascend a third steep learning curve. It will be as difficult as becoming really proficient at a trade. It's as challenging as becoming effective at managing and leading a construction company. Fortunately, for people who like learning, investment lore is compelling stuff. As you master it, you will be able to confidently move toward financial freedom.

Investment Literacy I: Principles

Earlier I told you about the general contractor who would not spend a few bucks on a book to educate himself about business management. He knew all that stuff, he said. Maybe you will recall his results: His wife got tired of taking care of his office work and dumped him. His construction company went under.

He personifies what I call the "arrogance of ignorance." It's the tendency to underestimate the amount you don't know about an enterprise, overvalue whatever knowledge you do have, and conclude that you know exactly what you are doing. Arrogant ignorance is deadly in investing. It's a fast track to losing a lot of money.

In investing, as in the trades and the construction business, you need to know what you are doing. You don't have to become a finance professional. You do have to acquire basic financial literacy. Fortunately, the essential knowledge is readily available. It can be found in the writings of a small group of professional investors.

Foremost among the investment sages is Ben Graham, author of *The Intelligent Investor* and the mentor of the legendary investor Warren Buffett. Close behind Graham is John Bogle, the founder of the giant financial firm Vanguard and author of several books on mutual funds – businesses which create portfolios of stocks, bonds, and other financial securities and sell shares of the portfolio to investors like you and me.

Both Graham and Bogle did their work decades ago. I have yet to encounter anyone of equal wisdom and of equal value to us construction pros who seek financial freedom. There are, however, investment professionals who have built on Graham and Bogle and been successful over a long term. They too have something useful to teach us. You will encounter a few of them in this and the following chapters. All the sages do invest primarily in the stock and bond markets. The principles they teach are equally sound for other markets, including real estate.

Before we get to certain core principles of investing, a few cautionary notes: First, for anyone who wants to travel the path to financial independence, the challenge is not finding sound investment guidance. The challenge lies in adhering to it and not becoming distracted by the myriad hustlers who pollute the financial world.

Once they get wind of your interest in investment, the hustlers bombard you with come-ons. They'll be popping up and pitching you on YouTube. They will be sending you invitations to "free" dinners – that you pay for with the hours of your time spent listening to their sales pitch. The hustlers claim they have the inside track to riches. They claim great successes – but won't offer you independent reviews of their performance. They never do mention their failures.

They proclaim how eager they are to share their secret sauce with you.

There are no secrets about investing, not for stocks, not for bonds, not for real estate, not for anything. The foundational knowledge is anything but secret. It has long been published in the books of Graham and Bogle.

A second caution: We can learn from the sages of the investment world. But it is generally unwise to attempt to match their performance. A few financial pros do achieve what is termed "alpha." That is, they "outperform" the markets. The valuation of investments they select rises substantially more quickly that the overall valuation of whatever market they happen to be investing in.

For example, Warren Buffett created a company, Berkshire Hathaway, which invested in the stocks and bonds of large corporations and purchased smaller companies outright. For decades, the value of Berkshire Hathaway rose substantially faster than the value of a mutual fund that simply held shares of all of the five hundred most highly valued U.S. corporations (i.e., the Standard and Poor 500, or S&P 500 for short). That's outperformance. That is achieving alpha.

Outperformance is unusual. By and large, even professional money managers provide their clients with underperformance over the long term. Yes, the pros who relentlessly buy and sell and maneuver in pursuit of alpha generally do worse by their clients than investors who passively hold onto a simple S&P 500 fund.

The chance that you or I, with our attention largely focused on construction, will outperform markets is somewhere south of zero. Trying to keep up with the Buffets of the world is not a part-time job or a hobby. If we try to outperform, the likelihood is that we will, instead, underperform, maybe badly. When you try for the big killing, there is a good chance you will, instead, shoot yourself in both feet.

After becoming intrigued with investing, I spent a few years trying for outperformance myself. I read Graham's book four times. I read everything Warren Buffett had said or published. I took a course in financial analysis at one of the best business schools in the world.

I thought I was ready to go. I began investing in the stocks of a series of companies. Among them was Armstrong World Industries (AWI), a longtime manufacturer of construction materials. My kind of investment, right? Investment gurus advise, "Invest in what you know." I know construction materials.

I analyzed AWI's financial statements. The company looked to be financially strong. It had low debt relative to its assets. It steadily earned a profit and paid its investors substantial dividends year after year. The stock looked to be priced at a bargain level. I saw a promising upside. Surely an investment in AWI would greatly increase in value when the market evaluated the stock properly.

AWI was cheap for a reason. I saw the reason. It was mentioned in the company's financial reports. The company had a huge asbestos lawsuit hanging over its head. Too eager to get underway as a hotshot investor, I ignored the warning. The settlement of the suit put AWI into bankruptcy. The bankruptcy wiped out my investment.

Over the decades, a few of my investments in stocks of individual companies have outperformed the S&P 500. Others have lagged behind it. I have not calculated my overall results down to the last dollar. It appears to me that at best I kept pace with the 500. Realizing even those anemic results took a huge amount of study and research. Since time is money, the bottom line is that I have underperformed financially.

After a couple of years of putting a great deal of time into investment, I decided there were better ways to spend my life. I figured I would have more fun and do more for my community as a construction pro than by attempting to become an alpha investor. I was definitely right about the fun. Warren Buffett loves sitting in his office and absorbing business news and financial analysis all day. I did not.

I moved to investments that are designed to simply match market performance and require very little attention. We will be discussing such investments in Part IV. Here it is enough to emphasize that matching market performance over the long term is not bad. In fact, historically, it results in highly desirable outcomes.

Ironically, investing in simple low-cost mutual funds that aim simply to match market performance is exactly what Warren Buffett advises his family members to do. Don't chase alpha, he says. Just steadily invest in the U.S. and world economy via those simple mutual funds. You will do great, he says. He's right. We'll look at the numbers later.

Investing, whether in stocks or real estate or some other market, is not a competitive sport. You do not have to outscore everyone else to win. Investing for financial freedom is more like keeping up a steady pace on a long hike in order to get to a good place.

The most important of the principles for successful investing can be expressed in three words: margin of safety. Those are Ben Graham's words. He came up with them when challenged to distill his advice on investing down to a short phrase.

Fail to invest with a margin of safety and you have made an error similar to one that construction pros often make in the management of their companies. Enticed by a mirage of huge profits or hoping to take a great leap forward with their businesses, they take on a job that their company is not ready to do. They step beyond the boundaries of safety. They fall over a cliff.

When construction pros ignore margin of safety in bidding for work, their mistake is likely, in good part, undercharging for the work. With investing, the mistake is the reverse. It is paying too much. Ben Graham explains: "The margin of safety is always dependent upon the price paid. It will be large at a low price, small at some higher price, and non-existent at some still higher price."

Investing with margin of safety requires that you don't merely take risk. You manage and minimize it. You strive to invest in situations where heads, you win; tails you don't lose that much. Keeping in mind Graham's observation about price, you buy at reasonable (or better) prices. In other words, to maintain margin of safety you hold back from buying in booming markets that inflate prices to risky levels.

You don't buy when the chances of prices sliding downward are much greater than the likelihood of their ascending. For example, say that home prices have gotten so high few people can afford homes; and should mortgage rates rise, almost no one will be able to afford them until prices collapse. In that case, you'd have little margin of safety if you went shopping for a rental property. You wait till you can get a better price.

That's obvious, right, just common sense? Doesn't any sensible person always look for a good price when buying something? Not investors, or at least a great many of them. Too often, they do the reverse. They flock to an investment marketplace when prices are rising steeply. They don't want to miss out. They flee the market when prices drop precipitously, when the markets are holding a fire sale.

As we approached the year 2000, corporate earnings were rising as the United States emerged from a recession. Interest in the stock market revived and then intensified. Stock prices rose. Meanwhile, high tech and the internet had moved forcefully into our daily lives.

Stock buyers were gripped by a compelling narrative (as they so often are during periods of steeply rising valuations of any asset class). The story was: We were entering a new millennium equipped with extraordinary new technology. Surely a new era of limitless economic possibilities was dawning. Enthralled by the story, investors became euphoric. The prices of stocks, especially those of internet companies, soared.

The stock of one internet company in particular attracted my attention. It had never made a profit nor even yet brought a product to market. Yet investors were bidding up its price to stake their claim in the new era.

The founder of the company was a man with a remarkable gift for hype and salesmanship. He had once been a much-envied member of my builders' group, growing his sales volume at a stunning rate. That was before his construction business went bankrupt, and he reinvented himself as an internet entrepreneur. As the price of the stock in his new internet company climbed, the value of his own shares exceeded a billion dollars.

A short time later, the twentieth century gave way to the twenty-first. Disappointingly, the new century did not turn out to be an economic utopia. The euphoria about a new era began to subside. The stock market began to deflate.

Stock prices in general plunged downward at an accelerating rate for three years. Technology stocks led the way down, losing close to 90 percent of their value. The stock of the internet firm founded by the former builder became worthless. He was bankrupt again.

Investors who had bought during the giddy "new era" days lost a great deal of money. Holders of shares in the former builder's company lost their entire investment. As Ben Graham pointed out, there's little margin of safety when you buy at high prices.

Buying with the maximum possible margin of safety is not possible. We cannot know just when the prices for stock or real estate or any other investment have hit rock bottom and pounce at that optimal moment. We can, however, determine reasonably good times to invest. For the major markets – real estate, stocks and bonds included – there are, as we will discuss in Part IV, metrics, i.e., quantifiable measurements, available. They enable us to determine whether we are getting at least an okay price and buying at an acceptable margin of safety.

That brings us to what, in my view, is the second fundamental principle of investing for the construction pro interested in reaching financial freedom.

When opportunities to invest with reasonable margin of safety do come along, invest you must. You can't just stack cash in your safe or in a savings account at the bank.

Cash may be beautiful stuff. You can use it to pay your living expenses and purchase fabulous construction equipment. It provides your business with a buffer against hard times. But as Ray Dalio, a professional investor with a remarkable record, puts it, in the long run "cash is trash."

Dalio's phrase can be off-putting for people who are savers rather than investors. But the fact is that over time savings lose purchasing power, occasionally over very short periods of time and at very high speed. Your cash might buy you a good hamburger the year you set it aside. Some years down the road it will barely buy the pickles and the bun.

Inflation is the villain. It steals away the purchasing power of savings. Inflation in any one year is likely to be so low we hardly notice it. In the United States it has run, on average, 3.25% percent a year since 1913. Its cumulative impact is enormous. At the 3.25% percent rate, twenty years from now, any cash you sock away today will buy you only half of what it will buy today.

Cash is not an investment. Once your company has the necessary capital reserves and cash is piling up in your investment bucket, you want to be on the lookout for opportunities to put the cash into actual investments, like real estate, stocks and bonds. The longer you wait, the further the cash is likely to degrade toward trash.

As you invest your cash, you will want to abide by a third fundamental principle of investing: Diversify your investments. Diversity is the handmaiden to margin of safety in investing just as it can be in agriculture. If you are a farmer and raise only a single crop, during a spate of bad years for that crop you may not have enough income to pay the expenses of running your farm. At the same time, the market value of the farm will likely go down. Similarly, if you are overconcentrated in one kind of investment – say a narrow segment of the stock market or real estate in a single town – the income from your investments can dry up when you hit a bad patch. At the same time, the market value of your holdings will likely drop sharply.

With a diversified portfolio, you can hit a period when several of your investments may suffer simultaneously. Chances are others will do okay. Some of your "crops" will be satisfactory even though others are wilting. With diversity you have a better chance of riding out a hard time in reasonably good shape. To invoke another farm-related analogy: You don't have all your eggs in one basket.

Ray Dalio presents a portfolio that exemplifies diversity. It contains a wide range of investments including stocks in companies of all sizes. It is called an "all-weather portfolio." It is designed to ride out rough economic times with only moderate loss in value, grow in value during better times, and pump out income during both. The portfolio of a construction pro focused on financial freedom might look quite different than the portfolio of a billionaire financial pro like Dalio. But the principle, building the portfolio for all kinds of weather via diversity, is as sound for us as it is for Ray Dalio.

There we have the bedrock principles of investing as I – not a financial pro by any means, but simply a construction guy who got past the point he had to work for economic reasons at an early age and has strengthened his position ever since – understand them: Invest you must, because cash eventually degrades into trash. Invest with margin of safety. Diversify to strengthen margin of safety.

Investment Literacy II: Practices

Maintain margin of safety. Don't just save cash, invest it. Diversify your investments.

Accompanying those fundamental principles are a few useful corollaries. Number One: Resist speculation. Going for the Hail Mary, acting on the hot tip about the can't-miss next big thing, that is not investing. It's gambling on the long shot.

Now and then, of course, we see someone succeed with a long shot. That can tempt us to make our own bets on an allegedly next big thing. Friends of mine made $5,000 bets on both Microsoft and Apple when they were just part of the pack of promising computer and software companies. Those bets have grown to millions of dollars.

Seeing that, I am sometimes tempted to look around for a few promising big bets myself. But I bear in mind that when my friends made their bets, they did so with only a small portion of their life savings. Heads came up. They won. Should tails have come up, they would not have been hurt all that much.

I have another friend who has spent his life repeatedly going for broke with everything he had. His result: he is broke. Every time I talk with him, he tells me about the new big play he is making. Any moment now, he says, he will be in a position to make philanthropy his new occupation. Meanwhile he shares an inexpensive apartment with a worn-out tennis pro and works as a security guard.

His results are not surprising. Ben Graham advised us half a century ago: "It is easy for me to tell you not to speculate. The hard thing will be for you to follow this advice. If you want to speculate, do so with your eyes open, knowing you will probably lose money in the end."

Speculators get excited by a perceived prospect of an outsize increase in market prices. They are inclined to jump into an escalating market with the hope of riding it to yet higher levels. Investors, on the other hand, like market collapses. They are focused on the present and longer-term earning power of an investment – rents from a rental, profit from a corporation, interest from a bond; for it is earnings that, in the long run, determine the value of an investment. Investors realize that down markets provide opportunities to buy at prices that are low relative to the amount of earnings their investments can realize.

Purchasing of gold is a much-favored form of financial speculation. Unlike investment in stocks, bonds, or real estate, gold does not offer earnings. It pays no dividends or interest and no rents. In fact, it produces negative cash flow because its owner must, one way or the other, pay to store it.

There are two reasons for buying gold. One is the belief that its price will go up so that it can be sold for profit. The other is the hope that the gold will act as a counterweight in a portfolio by increasing in value when other investments are suffering.

The first reason for owning gold is entirely speculative. The second is speculative but with prudence mixed in. Last time I looked, Ray Dalio's all-weather portfolio mentioned in the previous chapter was around 8 percent gold. Gold is included in the portfolio as a sort of ballast or insurance. It does tend to rise in value when other kinds of investments in the portfolio, stocks especially, decline.

Sometimes speculation in gold pays off. Over relatively short periods, gold has increased at a substantially faster rate than investments in other markets, including stocks. Over the long term it has lagged behind stocks by a staggering amount. One study reports on the results of investing a dollar in stocks versus gold in 1802. Two hundred and eleven years later, in 2013, the stock investment would have grown to an inflation adjusted $706,199, the gold investment to $4.50. And that, according to my own research, was after a hot streak for gold without precedent over the preceding century. Around a decade earlier, in 2003, the gold purchased for a dollar in 1802 was, adjusted for inflation, worth ninety-eight cents.

Purchase of gold, other than as ballast for a portfolio, is a bet by the purchaser that they can look into their crystal ball and perceive conditions that will foster a steep rise in the price of gold. As Ben Graham pointed out, buying gold had long been standard practice even during his day for people who distrust the economy. It still is.

On YouTube, as I write this paragraph, you can find "gold bugs" insisting that the economy is about to collapse, bragging about their collections of gold bars, prophesying extraordinary rises in the price of gold, and encouraging you to join in their speculation. You will find others enthusing over so-called "cryptocurrencies," another investment with no actual earning power. The initial crypto star, Bitcoin, became fashionable as I began this book. Now, today, while I am editing this chapter, its price is plunging and is over 50 percent off its high. Time will tell whether cryptos will ascend to untold heights, bottom at zero as did many internet stocks, or land somewhere between those extremes.

As you venture into the world of investing, you will likely find yourself encouraged to engage in a form of speculation known as "using other people's money." Use of that money – whether a bank's, a private lender's, or from a relative who entrusts their life savings to you – is praised as enabling "leverage."

In construction, using a lever, you seek to move more than you can with just your own muscle. In investing with leverage, you are seeking to lift up your financial results. For example, you make an offer of a $1,000,000 on an apartment building. The offer is accepted. You put down $100,000 of your own money. The remaining $900,000 you borrow. You may get it from a bank. You may get it from a private lender. You close the deal. Thereby, with use of someone else's money, you've acquired ownership of a property ten times the size of the one you could have moved into your portfolio using only your own $100,000.

All goes well for a time. You are able to raise rents and enjoy cash flow after making payments on your loan (i.e. mortgage), taxes, insurance and maintenance. You feel proud to be the owner of an apartment building. More exciting, the market value of the property rises steadily. At the end of a few years, its market value is $1,100,000. The bank still owns $900,000 worth of the apartment building (minus whatever amount of the mortgage you have paid off). You now have, along with the income from rents, over $200,000 equity in the building – i.e., your initial investment of $100,000 plus the $100,000 increase in value and your mortgage paydown. You've more than doubled your money. That's leverage working nicely.

Financial leverage is not, however, exactly parallel to the use of a lever on a construction job. Maybe it has happened, but I've never heard of anyone getting flipped in the air because they tried to lever up too big a load on a job site. Financial leverage can readily flip you upside down.

For example, say the economy tanks a few years after you buy that apartment building. Apartment vacancy rates rise. Some of the apartments in your building sit empty. Now, instead of enjoying cash flow, you are taking in less in rents than you must pay out for mortgage and other expenses. If things get really bad, you will be hemorrhaging cash.

Meanwhile, property values plunge. The value of your apartment building drops by 25 percent, i.e., by $275,000 (1,100,00 × 25 percent = 275,000). Your apartment building's market value has been reduced to $825.000 (1,100,000 – 275,000 = 825,000). You have lost your initial deposit of $100,000, your earlier gain of $100,000, and an additional

$75,000. Your apartment building is now worth $75,000 less than the nearly $900,000 you still owe your lender. In the parlance of the financial world, your investment is "underwater." Millions of property owners found themselves far underwater during the financial crises that began in 2007.

When things go south with leverage, you lose your investment and also lose money you got from "other people." You remain obliged to pay it back to them. Rather than amplifying gains with leverage, you have put yourself deep in a hole.

"Speculation" has many definitions. They include "conjecture that is impossible to verify," "gambling," and "adventure." Speculation is fun until it's not.

Avoidance of speculation does not, of course, eliminate risk. Any investment involves some measure of risk. No investment is a sure thing. You are looking to the future and banking on good results when you invest. Temporary setbacks are near inevitable. Market valuations are regularly knocked down by historical events like the financial crises of 2007 and the onset of a pandemic in 2020.

No matter how intent you are on maintaining your margin of safety, you can make mistakes in investing. Warren Buffett makes mistakes. He put billions into Kraft-Heinz and promptly lost billions. He freely admits he made the mistake his teacher Ben Graham warned of. He failed to maintain margin of safety by paying too high a price for the food company.

I make mistakes, as with my investment in AWI. I bought a good business but paid too high a price for one threatened by massive lawsuits. (In the case of my mistake, the right price turned out to be $0 since AWI went bankrupt and the stock became worthless. Buffett's stumble was not quite that bad.)

Because both market risk and the risk of making mistakes is built into investing, you must work to reduce risk in order to maintain a margin of safety. The point is not to eliminate risk but to dilute it. As one financial professional put it, lowering risk is the key to enjoying reward.

We have now touched on several ways of lowering risk: Not buying into stories about easy riches. Avoiding or at least minimizing speculative investments based on the mere conjecture, impossible to verify, that the valuation of an investment has nowhere to go but higher and higher. Making investments that have actual long-term earning power and largely avoiding those that do not. Holding back when market prices are soaring upwards and instead buying in down markets when there is a sale on.

Traveling the road to financial freedom does not require excess risk taking. That powerful force called "compounding" that we have alluded to in earlier chapters can propel you forward without your having to take undue risk.

An example will illustrate the force of compounding. You make a $1,000 investment. Your investment gains value at an average rate of 8 percent annually, an historically moderate after-tax rate for stocks.

After one year of 8 percent growth the $1,000 has become $1,080 (1,000 × 8 percent = 80; 1,000 + 80 = 1080). After two years, the initial investment has grown to $1,167 (1,080 × 8 percent = $87; 1,080 + 87 = 1167). After three years, to $1,260. And so on, until after twenty years of compounding the $1,000 has grown to $4,660, and after forty years to $22,000.

The power of the compounding derives from the fact that the 8 percent annual growth does not apply only to the initial $1,000 investment. Rather, each year it is also applied to all the gains over all the preceding years. In the third year of our above example, the 8 percent is applied not to $1,000 but to $1,167. After twenty years it would be applied to $4,660 for a gain of $373. That's equivalent to a 37 percent gain on the initial $1,000 investment.

A caveat here, an important one, what you might think of as fine print you overlook at your peril: Our above example is prettier than reality. It implies a steady, unvarying upward rise in the value of the investment. The actuality is likely to be much bumpier. The value of the investment may well go sharply up some years, steeply down in others, hardly move at all in yet others, and in some years be close to the average rate of growth. Furthermore, if you invested your $1,000 at a time when the market was very high, thereby ignoring margin of safety, and the market soon crashed, your gains could be seriously compromised for a very long while.

That said, there's good news as well. In investing, time is on your side. The longer you stay invested, the better your chances of riding out a down market – at least with a broadly diversified portfolio and assuming historical patterns continue.

Moreover, the earlier you start investing, the better your results are likely to be. Here's a variation on an oft-recited parable that drives the point home: Alexandria began investing $1,000 a month in a tax-protected retirement account at age twenty-five. She continued putting in $1,000 a month until she was thirty-five. Peter started investing $1,000 a month at age thirty-five and continued till age forty-five.

Both Alexandria and Peter left their investments in place and let them grow until they were sixty-five. Peter's investment grew to $750,000, Alexandria's to a million and a half. Alexandria and Peter had invested the same amount of money for the same length of time, $1,000 a month for ten years. Because she started a decade earlier, Alexandria's return was double Peter's.

As forceful as compounding is, we do need to temper our enthusiasm for it. There are forces at work that restrain the actual results compounding can deliver.

Those forces are sometimes ignored by the financial evangelists who populate the airwaves and social media. One such person, writing in 2007, urged a young couple with a moderate income to tighten their belt, pay off student loans and other debts, and thereby free up $1,850 a month for investment in stocks.

The evangelist projects that the investment will grow via "the miracle of compounding" into a million-dollar stock portfolio in fifteen years and to $5 million in twenty-eight years. He is holding out a promise that a young couple with modest income can, thanks to compounding, become seriously wealthy by their senior years.

These projections, however, assume a highly optimistic growth rate for the investments of 13 percent annually. Assume instead a more realistic growth rate of 10 percent, the historical average for a highly diversified all-stock portfolio. In that case, the couple's investment would grow not to $5 million but to around $3 million.

Now suppose the couple, instead of going for the all-stock portfolio, opted for investments along the lines of the all-weather portfolio described in the previous chapter. In that case, at historically average rates, their investments would grow at around 8 percent annually. And over twenty-eight years their wealth would grow to about two million dollars, not five million.

Their prospects look even less miraculous when we take into account the inevitable reality of taxes and inflation. I will spare you the math. With both taxes and inflation factored in, the annual average rate of gain in the couple's portfolio won't come close to 8 percent, much less 13 percent. In *real dollars*, it would be around 5 percent.

Rather than magically becoming $5 million, the couple's investments, if made in the diversified all-stock portfolio, would grow in real dollars to about $1.3 million. If placed in the all-weather portfolio their real dollar harvest would be around $1 million. That's one fifth of what the evangelist encouraged them to look forward to. They will have built a comforting retirement nest egg but be far from rich. That's the reality.

For those of us interested in achieving and maintaining financial freedom, it is critical to stay in touch with reality. We must, just as in running a construction business, tamp down thinking errors. For many who start down the road to financial freedom, that may be the toughest of all practices to adhere to.

Warren Buffett and Ben Graham both caution us that in investing our worst enemy is likely to be the noise inside our heads. Buffett suggests that the key to successful investing is not unusual smarts but having the right temperament. It's the calm and patience that allows us to ignore crazy market fluctuations, fads, and frenzy – to instead steadily make sensible investments and stick with them.

Graham famously compared the movements of the markets to a person – "Mr. Market" he affectionately calls him – whom today we would describe as manic-depressive. At times Mr. Market is so enthusiastic and over-confident that he buys at irrationally inflated prices. At others, he is so morose and gloomy he will sell at pathetically low prices (and pass up the opportunity to buy at fire-sale prices).

It requires considerable self-control, Graham emphasizes, for an investor to just stand aside during the manic phase and to invest during despondent markets. During the manic phase, we may feel compelled to get in on the action. We are fearful of missing out. When Mr. Market turns morose, gloom and fear can infect even seasoned financial professionals.

A certain accountant who serves the construction industry had built up a substantial portfolio of stocks over decades of hard work. When Mr. Market turned gloomy during a recession and stock prices tumbled, the accountant became terrified of "losing everything" and sold all his stocks. He did not buy back into the market till prices had recovered substantially. His fear-infected thinking had led him to sell at a low price and purchase at a much higher one.

As investors, rather than going along with Mr. Market, we want to avoid investing when he is in a manic mood. Ideally, we want to be making investments when he is in a depressive selling mood and is holding a fire sale. At the very least. we want to invest when Mr. Market is being sensible with his valuations of assets.

Fortunately, we have available means and tools for determining when we can make our investments with reasonable or better margin of safety. They will also help us decide when we should hold off investing (or perhaps even sell off assets that have become extravagantly overpriced). They enable us to rationally deploy the capital we have stored up in our investment buckets.

Deploying Capital

Financial markets have been going through booms followed by busts for centuries. Knowledge of their history helps us to ride out market turbulence and improve our chances of deploying the cash in our investment buckets successfully. Knowledge gives us perspective. It enables us to step back during manic markets, resist the frenzy, and avoid buying at inflated prices. We have observed how that has worked out for investors in the past.

The first speculative financial market seems to have been a craze for investing in tulips that arose in the Dutch Republic in 1637. The asking price for the most prized tulips climbed to ten times the annual salary of a skilled carpenter.

Flash-forward to the 1960s. A college student named Williams began selling mobile homes and incorporated his business. Then he jumped into franchising – a new development that mesmerized stock buyers much as the internet would three decades later – and offered stock in his corporation to the public. Long story short, the stock price promptly doubled after its initial public offering (IPO). Williams expanded his corporation into vaguely related fields. His corporation hemorrhaged cash, ran through its capital reserves, went heavily into debt, and declared bankruptcy twenty-one months after the IPO.

There were numerous speculative bubbles between the tulip craze and the franchising excitement. They keep on coming. We touched on two relatively recent ones in earlier chapters: the internet-centered speculation of the late 1990s and the extravagant increases in real estate valuations that preceded the mortgage crisis and the crash of 2007. With the collapse of each of those bubbles, masses of people lost vast amounts of money.

That poses a question: How do you avoid speculative bubbles? How do you know when to step back from investing? How do you know to bide your time, and keep your cash in your bucket till a more opportune moment?

It is not easy to know just when the valuation of a particular stock or mutual fund or some other type of asset, whether it's gold or real estate or cryptocurrency, begins acceleration to irrational heights. The rise can begin innocuously. In the marketplace for stocks, for example, the initial run-up in prices may start quietly and for sound reasons. An economic recession has subsided. Corporate earnings are rising. Corporations are increasing their payouts to stockholders.

So far, okay. But what sometimes follows is, to borrow a term from the economist Robert Shiller, an unhealthy "feedback loop." The improvement in corporate performance attracts investors, who bid up the price of stocks, thereby rousing interest among more investors, who bid prices up further, attracting yet more investors, and so on. Interest grows into widespread enthusiasm, which grows into intense excitement about fortunes to be made, which can amplify into an actual frenzy and a grossly inflated speculative bubble.

From my own experience – which includes decades of hands-on investing, observing the behavior of friends and neighbors, and reading – I have come to think there is a tip-off that markets have gone berserk. It's there in the conversations and commentaries you encounter on the street and in the media.

You hear talk of a "new era." You hear that we are at the threshold of prosperity like no one has ever seen before. That we have entered a moment of unprecedented historical change. That forces are in play that make it impossible for asset prices to decline while other forces will push them ever higher – or alternately, that while some assets are doomed, others will appreciate astronomically. You will, especially, hear the phrase, or something akin to it: "Times are different now."

You will receive that wisdom from people at your favorite coffee shop or pub. You will hear it trumpeted by media pundits, including authors of hot, best-selling books. One classic example: In 1999, a journalist and a scholar teamed up to write a book titled *Dow 36,000*. The stock market, they argued, was undervalued. They forecast an imminent rise of 350 percent. Immediately after publication of the book, the stock market collapsed. The Dow (short for Dow Jones Industrial Average, a measure of the market price of the stocks of thirty large U.S. companies) dropped below 8,000.

A knowledge of the history of markets, of their tendency to enter periods of wild speculation accompanied by outsize claims, can help us remain patient during the bubbles. It can help us resist paying those high prices that so severely compromise margin of safety. We're more able to "just stand there and not do anything," as Warren Buffett advises, and wait for more opportune moments to invest.

While a knowledge of history can provide us with overall guidance in our investment decisions, we need more precise instruments as well. We need mathematical means for determining when and how to deploy our investment capital. Fortunately, we have them. We have available metrics, measurements, and methods. They enable us to size up markets, recognize the excessively inflated ones and those offering reasonable or even very attractive prices.

The most sophisticated of these tools is called "discounting to present day value (PV)." In the "Tools" section at the end of this book you'll find a listing for a web article which explains the method fully and goes into the math. For here it will be enough to take a jargon-free look at the underlying concept.

"Present value" refers to the value of an asset at the present time, i.e., today. But note, please, that here "value" does not mean "market price." Rather, the PV of an investment is determined by analyzing its potential for generating future earnings. That is, investment x is determined to have a certain dollar value today based on the likelihood of its earning y dollars in the future.

The present value may be lower or higher than the price assigned by a market. For example, a rental house might, after present value analysis, be assigned a value of $200,000. In a heated-up economy with demand for houses at high levels, it might be priced at and sell for $300,000. During a severe recession, with demand for housing collapsed, the house could become available for $150,000.

Similarly with stocks: An analysis might peg the PV of a company's stock at forty dollars. During a manic market it might be priced at sixty dollars. In a gloomy market it might fall to twenty-five dollars or less.

In short, PV does not equal market price. It is not determined by the investing public's opinion of the worth of an investment. You determine it mathematically in order to make decisions about deployment of capital rationally, rather than on the basis of guesswork or emotion, whether enthusiasm or fear.

When you set out to determine PV, you are attempting to answer one question in order to successfully ask and answer another. The first question is: If I make this investment, how much is it likely to earn me in the future? With the first question answered, you can move on to the second question: Are those likely earnings attractive enough that I should make the investment?

For our purposes as construction pros seeking financial freedom, PV calculation is more approachable if we first look at it as a way of sizing up a potential real estate investment (even though in financial discussions it is typically brought up in connection with stock investing).

Say that real estate markets are down. You think it may be good time to invest in a rental property. You find a house that you can afford to purchase and renovate with the cash you have in your investment bucket.

To figure PV for the property, you conservatively project annual rents. You allow for periods of vacancy. You allow for moderate increases in rents, in line with those that you have determined to have been typical for the town where the property is located.

You also project all your costs. You allow for insurance and taxes. Importantly, you also allow for maintenance and for management, even if you plan on doing that work yourself. (Just as any work you do in your construction business should be accounted for as a cost, work you do in connection with an investment is a cost of investing.) Subtracting costs from rents, you come up with an expected annual income from the property.

You then figure that the first year you own the property your income will amount to 4 percent of the amount you expect to have to pay for the property. You figure that ten years down the road, after moderate annual rent increases, you will be at 6 percent and thereafter be able to further increase income.

You have now answered the first question: How much can I reasonably expect to earn from an investment in the property? With that answer in hand, you can move on to the second question: Are the potential earnings good enough to justify an investment in the property? In other words, is the present value of the property high enough to justify my buying it at the price I would have to pay for it?

To determine whether an investment is attractive, its potential earnings can be compared to those of a nearly risk-free investment. Typically, that would be a U.S. government bond that pays a fixed amount of interest annually. If the future return of an investment is expected to be less than or even the same as the return on the bond, then the investment is not attractive.

After all, why take the greater risk associated with a real estate investment for no greater return than that promised by the nearly risk-free investment in a U.S. bond? On the other hand, if the return on the real estate investment seems likely to be significantly better than that of the bond, you may want to go for it.

Let's take a look at an example with numbers. You spot a house for sale in an up-and-coming neighborhood. You do a thorough estimate and project that you can purchase and thoroughly renovate the house for $200,000. You figure that you will initially be able to realize a net income of 4 percent of the $200,000, or $8,000 a year, and that the income will gradually climb to 6 percent, or $12,000 a year, after a decade.

On the other hand, U.S. bonds are yielding historic lows. If you buy a ten-year bond you will be able to get only 2 percent. Furthermore, the property offers promising possibilities – for tax shelter, for development, for appreciation in value – of the kind that we will go into in some detail in our coming chapters on investing in real estate.

With all considerations figured in, the house looks to be a promising investment. Its present value, namely the likely future earnings it will bring you, is substantially better than that of the ten-year bond. Even if the possibilities beyond rental income do not materialize, you will likely get more bang for your buck with purchase of the property than by buying a bond.

The calculation of present value for stocks aims to answer the same questions that we addressed in our paragraphs about a real estate investment. Is investment in this stock, or in a bunch of stocks bundled up in a mutual fund, worthwhile, given what I would have to pay for it today? Is it a good buy, a great buy, or a bad one compared to a relatively risk-free investment like a U.S. bond?

Here's a simplified example (free of the heavy-duty math a pro stock analyst would likely use) of the decision making involved. Say that it is early 2021. Construction is booming. Profits are piling up in your investment bucket.

Ray Dalio's words are ringing in your ears; you don't want to let that cash just sit there and slowly turn into trash due to the impact of inflation and taxes. You look at real estate investments. Prices are too high. You calculate that they greatly exceed present value.

You decide to consider adding to your portfolio of stock mutual funds. Specifically, you look at the S&P 500 fund offered by Vanguard, the financial company founded by John Bogle. You see that the fund is paying out to its shareholders a dividend equal to 2 percent of its share price. The U.S. ten-year bond is yielding only 1.4 percent

At those numbers, the investment in the mutual fund looks relatively attractive. Still, you hesitate. Like real estate, the stock market has been soaring. It's into bubble territory, in the opinion of some students of market history. If it crashes, the valuation of the 500 fund will go down with it. You will lose, at least temporarily, a good deal of any investment you make in the fund.

On the other hand, a commentator you respect has suggested that the S&P 500 is not overvalued. In his opinion, present value for the 500 mutual fund pencils out. Not only does the dividend exceed the yield on the ten-year bond, but companies within the 500 are enjoying additional earnings they don't pay out as dividends. The companies are ploughing those earnings back into their own operations, increasing their value and, thereby, the value of your investment.

All in all, you decide, investment in the S&P 500 fund would be rational. Over the long term it should work out. There's a good chance dividends will gradually rise above their current 2 percent level. There is, additionally, a good chance the fund will rise in value over the long term, even if it drops for a while. The fund appears to have sufficient present value to make it a reasonable investment.

Present value calculation is worthwhile because it allows us to set aside emotion. It protects us from getting swept up in Mr. Market's manic-depressive cycle. We make our investments on the basis of a rational and mathematical calculation.

Like present value calculation, another investment technique, namely "dollar cost averaging" (DCA), helps you set aside emotion when deploying capital. If you have the discipline to stick with it, DCA can help you to avoid bouncing between fear in down markets and overeagerness in manic markets. It enables you to invest rationally over the long term. It has the additional advantage of being simple (a lot simpler than present value calculation), almost mechanical.

To employ dollar cost averaging, you make a series of investments at regular intervals regardless of market prices. Yes, some of your investments may be at high prices. But others will likely be at medium and low prices. Chances are that over time the prices you pay will average out satisfactorily.

An example from stock investing will explain: You commit to investing a thousand dollars in shares of a stock mutual fund every May 21st for five years. During the first year, the market is moderately priced when you invest. Your shares cost you $100 each. During the second year, Mr. Market got depressed, and your shares cost you only $50. During the third year, Mr. Market recovered somewhat and your shares cost you $75. The fourth year, Mr. Market slid over into manic exuberance. Your shares cost $200. In the fifth year Mr. Market returned to sanity. You were able to buy shares once again for $100.

You might assume, as I would have when I first learned about dollar cost averaging, that your average cost per share over the five years was $105. After all, your annual costs per of share of $100 + $50 + $75 + $200 + $100 equals $525. And $525 divided by 5 is equal to $105.

In actuality, your average cost is not $105. It's only $86! Why? Because during the first year when the price averaged $100, you received ten shares for your $1,000 (1,000 ÷ 100 = 10). When the price was $50 you got twenty shares (1,000 ÷ 50 = 20). At $75 you purchased thirteen shares; at $200 just five shares; and in the fifth year, with the price of shares back to $100, you again received ten shares. All told, you have purchased fifty-eight shares for $5,000 (10 + 20 + 13 + 5 + 10 = 58). Your average price per share is $86 because $5,000 ÷ 58 shares = $86.

You are buying at a satisfactory average price. It is well above the market low of $50 but far below the market high of $200 per share. It is significantly below the $100 valuation that recurs at the end of the fifth year.

You have a decent if not spectacular gain on your initial investment; the shares for which you paid an average of $86 are now worth $100. Additionally, you have received dividend payments during the five years that you have been investing the mutual fund. All told, you have invested without emotion, but steadily, mathematically, and done alright.

Something akin to dollar cost averaging *could* be used for building up a real estate portfolio. You commit to buying a property periodically, at say three-year intervals. You then have a fair chance of buying at a range of market prices, for the price of real estate does fluctuate. Your average price over time *may* turn out to be satisfactory.

I emphasize "could" and "may" because there are no guarantees here, just as there are none with any form of or method of investing. Additionally, you can't divide and spread out your purchases of real estate as readily as you can with stock investments (which you can and probably would make monthly rather than annually as in our example above), so your risk is more concentrated.

To protect yourself, you may find it best to hit the pause button when you are unable to find a property that provides a positive cash flow, i.e., income that is greater than your expenses. If you proceed to invest without positive cash flow, you are treading into pure speculation. You are steadily losing money on your investment in hope of some future gain resulting from a future rise in real estate values.

For the investor who can stay with it, dollar cost averaging helps to enable investing with margin of safety. It safeguards against going whole hog into manic markets. It mitigates the danger of backing away from down markets because they may go lower yet. It requires steadfastness, but does not use much of your time. It may be the best investment method for construction pros wanting to work their way steadily toward financial independence.

As you go about deploying your capital and building up your investments, you may, from time to time, want advice. Unfortunately, there is a lot more of the wrong kind of advice than the right kind out there.

You should, of course, be leery of the help offered by the hustlers coming at you on social media. Friends are not likely to be a much better source of guidance, though you may be inclined to rely on them. A study of investors indicated that 94 percent relied on friends as their primary source of guidance. The problem with relying on friends is that they may get caught up in the excess enthusiasm of manic markets or the gloom of down markets and pull you into destructive feedback loops.

Unfortunately, the credentialed investment pros you might assume would be a better source of guidance than folks in your personal network often are not.

According to one study, in 1999, as the stock market ascended to crazy heights and its collapse approached, only 15 percent of professional market analysts urged investors to sell; 70 percent said buy. Good grief!

During the stock market crash of 2020, investment analysts at a major bank predicted that the S&P 500 would gradually ascend to 2,700 by the year's end. Another veteran financial advisor, a man who oversees half a dozen offices that manage the savings of retirees, was also making predictions. He cautioned that the S&P should fall to 1,800 or less before the year was out. In fact, as 2020 came to an end, the market had risen to around 3,800.

Equally dubious as sources of investment guidance are superstar fund managers – women and men that you see celebrated in the media for the striking results they have achieved over a year or a few years.

As I write this book, one such superstar is getting a great deal of attention. Her name is Cathie Woods. A mutual fund she runs, and in which you can buy shares, quadrupled the gains of the S&P 500 from 2017 to 2021, streaking upward at dizzying speed during 2020. People who invested in her fund four years previously and stayed with their investment had enjoyed gains of near 900 percent. Woods had turned each of their dollars into nine dollars.

Woods argues that "this is a different time." We are, she argues persuasively, in a moment of unprecedented industrial revolution incorporating advances in robotics, finance, genomics, space exploration, and energy production and storage. Invest in the companies – the *right companies,* the ones that will dominate the revolution – and you will, she insists, see your investments grow rapidly.

You might be tempted to put your cash in the hands of Cathie Woods or whatever superstar next burns brightly. If so, be aware, you've got a challenge. You can't know who the superstars are until they have achieved stardom. And after a brief period of stardom they often decline into mediocrity. You are therefore likely to invest with them too late to benefit from their ascent, and instead not long before they begin their downward glide. You end up with losses or minimal gains instead of great ones.

Ben Graham once followed the performance of a selection of superstars in the years after they gained fame and were being heralded as geniuses in the press. They all declined into mediocrity, registering losses and underperforming the markets. Incidentally, Cathie Woods underperformed the S&P 500 during the year I completed writing this book.

If you can't count on reliable guidance from friends or professional investors, nor confidently put your faith in superstar money managers, who can you go to for advice on deploying your capital?

I am afraid my answer has to be redundant. Go to Ben Graham and John Bogle. Read them to get a handle on the fundamentals of investing: Maintaining margin of safety. Diversifying. Freeing yourself of emotion and investing rationally.

Figure present day value when making investments. Avoid speculative bubbles. Screw up your courage and invest in down markets. Or to keep things simple, just do dollar cost averaging and keep at it through the ups and downs.

Remember, as noted earlier, investing is not a competitive sport (though some folks treat it that way). To make the investments that will provide you with financial freedom, you don't need to swing for the fences and hit home runs. You just need to steadily make your way forward up the hill. As you climb you will want to rid yourself of the burdens, such as those we will turn our attention to now, that can slow your progress.

Friction, Debt, Max, and Taxes

Like a construction business, investing is burdened with expenses that can severely impair financial results if left unmanaged. In construction you have overhead – the expenses beyond the direct costs of the work itself, which you incur in order to deliver your product to your clients. In investing you have analogous expenses. They are termed "frictional" expenses. Like overhead expenses, they are charges associated with delivery of a product to its purchaser. But in this case, they are charges you pay for delivery of the product to yourself.

In real estate investing, you can be subjected to a series of frictional costs. A mortgage broker, if you elect to work with one, will charge you a fee to connect you to a loan provider. Next, you'll pay a fee for the privilege of applying for the loan. Once the application is approved, you can be required to pay "points," i.e., a percentage of the loan, in order to actually receive it.

You will also pay a fee to a title company to make sure your ownership of the property will not be compromised by someone else's claim. In some locales you'll have to pay a fee to the government for permission to make and record your purchase. All in all, those fees create a lot of friction. They rub away a substantial amount of capital.

In stock and bond investing, if you work with a broker to purchase individual stocks or bonds, you can get hit with a range of frictional costs from commissions to custodial fees. Frictional costs become especially severe if you hire out management of your portfolio to a financial advisor. Every year, they will take a substantial portion of the capital you entrust to them as a management fee, and that's after passing on to you all the other frictional costs of stock ownership.

Advisor fees vary widely. In recent years, some financial firms have begun offering robo-managers, digital services that automatically and with little human supervision periodically adjust your portfolio. The robotized management can cost as little as a few tenths of a percent annually. For an actual flesh and blood manager, fees of 1 to 2 percent of the market value of a portfolio are typical. Those percentages may look trivial at a glance. They are not.

Say, for example, that your manager's fee is 1 percent and that when you sign up for their services, you entrust them with $100,000 of your capital. In that case, over the next ten years you will pay them $10,000 to manage your $100,000 (100,000 × 1 percent × 10 = 10,000). At 2 percent, the managers will gobble up 20 percent, or one-fifth of the 100K over a decade.

Your fee will grow if your manager succeeds in growing the value of your portfolio (Not all managers do grow value. Some lose big chunks of the money their clients entrust to them even as they are collecting their substantial fees). If the manager who charges 1 percent grows your investment from $100K to $150K, your annual fee will grow from $1,000 to $1,500.

Maybe you are thinking, "That's not so bad, the guy made me 50 thousand bucks." However, over time even a 1 percent management charge can seriously retard your progress toward financial independence. Suppose your manager grew your stock portfolio at an annual rate of 9 percent *before* his fees. That means that after his 1 percent fee, the portfolio grew at 8 percent. Over twenty years at 8 percent, 100K grows into $466,000 (not adjusted for inflation). At 9 percent, it grows by an additional $94,000, to $560,000. In other words, over a couple of decades, that 1 percent cost you $94K.

The impact of friction reminds us that Ben Franklin's ancient advice remains valid: "Watch out for those small leaks; they can sink a big ship."

You won't be able to prevent all the leaking away of capital caused by frictional costs. You can, however, reduce them to the point they won't sink your ship or even cause it to ride noticeably lower in the water. We will discuss the specifics for both real estate and stock and bond investing in Part IV.

Debt burdens you with the one of the most corrosive of all frictional costs. Not only must you pay back the loan amount. You must pay interest charges that add greatly to or can even exceed the loan amount. Debt can sink you. If you fail to make the required payments on a mortgage, the lender can assume legal ownership of "your" building via foreclosure. The payments on other debt can burn so much cash they will severely compromise investment possibilities.

Consider the impact of payments for a new truck that was purchased to replace a serviceable older truck with ten years of life left in it. Assume that the payments for the new truck will run $700 a month for five years. Factor in higher insurance payments for the newer truck. Allow for greater costs of service and repairs for the older truck. All told, figure that the newer truck will cost you $600 a month more than the older truck.

Had the excess been invested instead in a stock fund… Well, I will leave it to you to do the math using the financial calculator listed in "Tools." My calculation assumes historically average growth in the value of the stock fund of around 10 percent. It assumes the investment is made inside a retirement account where the growth is sheltered from taxes until you begin withdrawing the money.

In that case, after five years, the money you saved and invested by maxing out the older truck rather than buying a new one will have grown to $45,000. If you leave that $45,000 to compound for another thirty years until you retire, your investment will have grown to roughly $300K. And that's in inflation-adjusted, *real* dollars. Plug small leaks and your ship will sail far. Ben Franklin did not say that. I did. But he could have.

It seems that for many folks, acquiring debt is easy and getting rid of debt is hard. With a mere momentary impulse, we take on debt. Shedding it can require persistent effort. We do have available two potent methods: the snowball and the avalanche.

With the snowball method, you start with your smallest debt. Each month you pay off the minimum required by the lender plus whatever additional amount you can afford. After paying off the smallest debt, you move to the next smallest, paying the minimum required plus the total amount you used to pay off the first debt. You move to the third debt, paying the minimum plus the amounts used to pay off the first and second debts. And so on, rolling down the debt mountain, until you have a big snowball and are attacking your largest debts.

With the avalanche method, you begin with the debt that has the highest interest rate. You work your way toward paying off the debt with the lowest interest rate. The avalanche method likely will save money more rapidly; you are getting rid of your most burdensome interest payments first. The snowball method, however, may be more potent. It starts you off with a readily achievable task, getting rid of a small debt, and helps you build momentum from there.

If you crave financial freedom and have debt, get rid of it. Choose the snowball or the avalanche. Free people are free of debt. Proverbs 22:7: "The borrower is servant to the lender."

As a construction pro, you do not need to take on debt. Generally speaking, construction companies are not capital-intensive businesses. With little cash, you can get up and running with a used truck, tools, and basic office equipment. Once you are underway, a fraction of your earnings will fund the necessary development of your business systems.

Going forward, you can build a lean and profitable company as discussed in Part II. Remain free of debt, hold back from taking excess pay for the work you do for your company, and you will be able to top up your capital reserves bucket, then steadily fill your investment bucket and make your investments. Easy? No. Worth the effort? I sure think so.

Max avoided debt as he built his company. At meetings of his builders' association, he sometimes heard others speak of their "relationship with my bank." They said it with pride, as if they were signifying sophistication. Max said to me, "I just don't get that. Why would anyone be proud of having to borrow money?"

Max never did borrow money. He figured if he could not afford to buy something for cash, then he'd just wait till he had the cash. Fact is, he rarely had to wait for long.

Max had steadily intensified the practices he instinctively gravitated toward or learned from his mentors: Employees first. Steadily improve efficiency on the jobsite. Bear down on quality. Throttle unnecessary off-site expenses. Sell at prices that are competitive because they include so little overhead, yet provide ample profit. Let your work do the talking. Emphasize taking care of your existing customers over seeking new ones. Enjoy their steady stream of references to people in their network.

The results for Max: He enjoyed running his company. He liked collaborating with his crew and trade partners and admired their work. He got satisfaction from moving projects from preconstruction cost analysis, value engineering, and contract negotiations through to foundation installation and finish work. His company pumped out cash.

It provided Max with enough pay to support a healthy though simple lifestyle and enough profit to gradually fill his capital reserve bucket, keep it full, and move on to steadily filling his investment bucket. He began investing, or what he thought was investing.

Max made a mistake, a big one as he would eventually realize. He fell prey to the arrogance of ignorance, assuming he was ready to embark on an enterprise he knew nothing about. He began investing without first learning how to invest.

He put his investment cash into certificates of deposit (CDs) during a time when interest rates were very high. The big interest payments looked juicy to him. Max failed to realize that inflation was also high and that the inflation plus taxes largely canceled out his interest income from the CDs. In real dollar terms, he was going nowhere. He acquired more dollars, but no more actual purchasing power from his "investments." For several years, Max just treaded water. He was really just a glorified saver, not an investor.

Max might have continued being merely a saver of cash indefinitely. A realtor friend persuaded him to invest in real estate. There too, Max blundered.

He purchased an old duplex. As a builder, he admired its Craftsman details. He was excited by the potential he saw for renovation and improvement. He had no idea how to evaluate the duplex as an investment nor the management responsibilities he was assuming. He did not know how to find reliable tenants for a worn building in a declining neighborhood. He was rocked by vacancies, by tenants who left their units filthy and roach-infested or who invented reasons for not paying rent, and, finally by one who was always late with rent, then delivered it in the form of change, the tips she had received at her job.

Frustrated, Max sold the duplex. Shortly afterward he jumped into a small apartment building. Again, he invested without analysis of potential costs versus benefits. Soon after he assumed ownership, the town in which the building was located passed a strict rent control law. Max saw that he would never be able to raise rents enough to recapture the costs of the renovation the building badly needed. He'd be forever trying to keep the place patched together and dealing with irritated tenants whose apartments were always needing repairs.

Max fled the apartment building, too, selling it to the first person who made an offer. Then he watched with chagrin as the new owner renovated the building, converted the legal status of the apartments to condominiums, and sold them off one at a time for solid profits.

Watching that, Max thought, "Sometimes you win; sometimes you learn. I don't know what the hell I am doing, so now before doing any more investing I am going to learn how to do it right."

Max hit the books, learning about many of the principles and methods we have discussed in this book, from margin of safety to dollar cost averaging. He began investing steadily. Over the years he acquired several good rental properties and built a stock and bond portfolio.

Because of his preference for frugality and lean operations, he zoomed in on frictional costs. He saw that they could severely impair investment results as readily as excess overhead could impair the financial outcomes for a construction company. Just as he had worked to restrain overhead costs, Max minimized frictional costs whenever and wherever he could.

There was, however, one frictional cost that Max could not avoid. Taxes! They seemed to be as inevitable as computer upgrades and change orders on a construction project. They took a big chunk of his interest when he was buying CDs. They soaked up large amounts of his rental income and of the dividends from his stocks and mutual funds. They claimed a substantial share of his gains when he sold an asset, whether a house or a stock that had risen in value.

Taxes are the biggest of the frictional costs we face in investing. But getting riled up about taxes does little good. That can lead to counterproductive decisions. Some folks get so agitated about taxes they will make horrible investment moves to avoid merely unpleasant taxation. A behavioral economist who works for a major financial firm reports that he regularly sees people spending more than a dollar to avoid a dollar in taxes.

Investing strictly for the purpose of avoiding taxes is foolish. Investing with tax consequences in mind makes sense. Fortunately, there are legal means for investing successfully while still accomplishing tax minimization. We will go into go into these specifics in some detail in Part IV.

For now, let's just note an antidote to tax pain that accompanies investment. It requires merely a change in perspective. You may not think much of it. One editor of this book refers to it as "smoke and mirrors." You might agree.

But please consider that changes in perspective can prevent thinking errors. Correction of thinking errors, of cognition, can prevent unproductive behavior. And, specifically, correction of thinking errors about tax friction can prevent investment errors.

The change in cognition that is an antidote to tax pain is simply this: A recognition that as you build your investment portfolio, your tax burden in *proportion to your income* may go up. But in *proportion to your assets* it can decline, even to trivial levels.

In other words, as your income rises, your taxes will rise as a percentage of the income. Your income goes up. You move to a higher tax bracket. Painful.

The reverse can be true with investments. As your investments grow, your taxes as a percentage of your assets can decline steeply. Comforting.

There's a simple reason for that. Assets – real estate and stocks especially – can compound in value. But that increase is generally not taxed unless you sell the asset.

Do you recall my friends, mentioned in an earlier chapter, who invested 5K in Microsoft and Apple and have watched the value of their shares rise into the increasing millions? They will not have to pay taxes on those gains until they sell the shares. Similarly (if not quite so dramatically), certain mutual funds have grown greatly in value without their owners having to pay taxes on the gains.

If you are a construction pro who is investing steadily, the likelihood is that the growth in the value of your investments is going too far outstrip the growth of your income, whether from construction, rents, dividends, or interest. Yes, your taxes as a proportion of that income will rise. But as the assets compound, the taxes, even though they are increasing, will likely become an ever-smaller proportion of the assets.

Once you recognize that, taxes may no longer seem like such a big deal. The change in perspective can forestall frantic and counterproductive efforts to avoid taxes. You won't be prone to spending more than a buck to avoid a buck in taxes.

That is just what happened for Max in his thinking about tax friction as he advanced in his career. Early on, he was taking home about $75,000 (in 2021 dollars). His taxes – state and federal income plus social security, sales taxes, and property tax on his home – amounted to some 25 percent of his income. On the other hand, he had barely begun to invest. His taxes were, for a while, even greater than the value of his assets; and for a longer while, they were large in proportion to his assets.

Flash forward to Max's situation in the years after he had learned how to invest and accumulated sufficient assets to be financially free. He no longer worked to earn money. He preferred working as a volunteer, mentoring younger people starting their own businesses and helping to build housing for people living on the streets. He did, however, enjoy a high income in the form of rents, dividends, and interest from his investments. It amounted to about $350,000 annually. Of that amount he paid some 40 percent, i.e., $150,000, in taxes.

Max grimaced when he had to write out his big checks for taxes. But he was not seriously troubled by the burden. He continued to live simply and recognized that his $200,000 after-tax income (350 – 150 = 200) was far more than he needed.

He also saw that his annual taxes, though a large percentage of his income, were a tiny portion of his assets – for due to the power of compounding they had grown enormously in value over the decades since he began building his portfolio. As a result, taxes, even though they had grown to be 40 percent of his large income, amounted to less than 1 percent of the value of his real estate, stocks and bonds.

Moreover, since he did not need extra money, Max rarely sold his assets. They continued to grow steadily, riding out market ups and downs and compounding ever more, so that taxes as a percentage of assets grew ever smaller.

"I don't really mind the taxes I have to pay," Max said to friends. "They make no dent to speak of in my financial freedom. The assets grow. They will pump out more income than I am ever likely to need."

To wealthy friends who bemoaned taxes, Max would repeat a comment made by a buddy who had immigrated to the United States from a much less fortunate nation and made himself wealthy: "We've got a good country here. It takes a lot of money to run it and protect it. We get a lot for our money. Police services. Roads. Schools. Parks. A safety net for our old age. Help for disabled folks. National defense. I feel good about contributing. Frankly, given our assets, we are not getting hit very hard."

Max, and others who build up sufficient assets to become financially free may someday be required to pay a percentage of their assets to support government programs. The authors of *The Millionaire Next Door* predicted decades ago that a wealth tax was coming to the United States. As of this writing, it has not arrived.

As of now, as a construction pro you are in a good position to invest with tax minimization. You can make your investments close to home. You can make them worldwide. Let's now turn our attention to the possibilities.

PART FOUR:
Anchoring Financial Freedom

- Investing in Your Construction Company
- Investing in Real Estate I: Possibilities
- Investing in Real Estate II: Execution
- Investing in the World Economy

Investing in Your Construction Company

In our discussions of investing as a path to financial freedom, I have so far focused on investments in real estate, stocks, and bonds. You may have been thinking, "What about investment in my own company? Could I not use my investment capital to strengthen my own company, then put it up for sale? Would the proceeds not provide for my financial freedom?"

Before taking a look at yes and no answers, let's emphasize that, of course, you will invest in your company. To begin with, you will, as Steve Nicholls, founder of a construction company that grew to employ eighty people, says, "make a huge investment of both spirit and time." You will build business systems. You will work to find people who want to practice their chosen craft at a high level, whether it's framing, plumbing, or keeping the books. You will steadily encourage and manifest respect toward them in all ways including with good pay.

You will invest money, at the very least, in tools and equipment, and perhaps in land, buildings, and vehicles. As you make those investments, you could hardly do better than to adopt the practices of Wally Staples, the owner of Wally J. Staples Builders, Inc., a design/build firm in Maine. Staples has steadily put money into his company. I have alluded to Staples in earlier chapters. You can learn more about his philosophy and operation from a podcast hosted by *Building Optimal Radio* (see "Resources").

Here I will mention a few striking aspects of Staples's practices as they relate to investment. Whenever he sees a piece of equipment that will allow his crews to work more safely or more efficiently or both, he buys it. He buys strictly for cash. He never borrows money and has no debt. He does not have to share his company's profits with outsiders; he makes no payments to any lender. Instead, he is able to spread profit around inside the company, providing employees with bonuses up to 14 percent of their annual wages.

Staples asks, "Who better to share your profits with than the great people who helped the company earn the profits." Not only does he share the profit. He educates his employees on methods and benefits of investing for the sake of their own future security. He demonstrates the possibilities to them with his own practices. With his share of his company's profits, Staples has purchased lots and built half a dozen rental houses while also diversifying into a portfolio of other investments.

Now in his early fifties, Staples is financially free. His company, with its capable and stable workforce and steady stream of profitable projects, has the earmarks of a salable business. He could sell the company and move to another phase of life if he wished to. But Staples has a passion for his work and enjoys it. He continues to invest in his company simply to make it better. He is not yet thinking about passing it on to other owners.

The owners of Winans Construction, on the other hand, invested in their company to strengthen it for the purpose of eventually selling it and retiring. As Paul Winans describes in his memoir, *The Remodeling Life*, he and his wife Nina decided they wanted to exit the construction business. They hired a consultant, under whose guidance they created a ten-year plan to get their company ready for sale, and methodically set about executing the plan.

Gradually they increased their profit margins. They became more selective about clients, seeking those who would pay a premium for their reliable services. They systematized all aspects of their company's work, creating what Paul calls "a road map of documents" that employees could rely upon when the owners were not around. Critically, they brought in people who could handle company management functions, including sales and estimating, so that the company was not dependent on Paul and Nina for a steady flow of work.

They tested their people and systems by absenting themselves from the company. Eventually they were leaving for three weeks at a time, with their employees under orders not to call them. After the decade of building their brand and strengthening the company, they listed it with a broker. He found them a buyer, and the Winanses completed their exit from the construction business.

Potential buyers of construction companies include people experienced in other businesses. They want to move into construction because they think it can be lucrative or satisfying work, or both. Buyers also include owners of construction companies who want to buy another firm as a way of expanding their customer base or getting into a new market. That was the case for my mentor, Deva Rajan, founder of Canyon Construction. Canyon had long focused on high-end residential work. Rajan expanded by purchasing a company that specialized in building improvements for a prominent university.

Finally, the buyer for a construction company might be an employee or group of employees. They may think that they can increase their income by becoming owners. Or they simply like their company's culture and want to continue on with it when the founder bows out. In fact, though there is no definitive data available, it appears that the majority of the buyers of small construction companies are employees.

Sometimes a buyer purchases a construction company with money from a lender or their own assets, and the owner gets paid in full at the time of sale. Sometimes the purchase is made with installment payments from the company's future profits.

If you are thinking of selling your company, be aware that the installment option can be hazardous. A company is sold. The buyer proceeds to mismanage it, damaging both its reputation and operations, and fails to make payments to the previous owner, who may then have to resume running the now impaired business. That does happen.

Often when a small construction company is sold to employees, the sale is made via a legal device called an "ESOP," an employee stock ownership plan. ESOPs are complex. "Resources" lists a website where you can learn about them in detail. Here it will be enough to note that setting up an ESOP is costly, requiring the hiring of specialists, including attorneys.

Once the attorneys have put the necessary legal structure in place, the ESOP can take a loan from a bank, using the proceeds to buy the company from its owner. With ownership assumed, the ESOP distributes shares to all the company's employees – not just to senior managers. As a result, the advocates of ESOPs believe, employee morale and loyalty are encouraged. Since they now have shares in the company and therefore get a share of its profits, all employees will, it is assumed, be motivated to work for its success.

If the employees actually are motivated and succeed in sustaining the company, that in turn can be a good thing for the owner. But not necessarily. Like installment sales, ESOPs can be hazardous for owners. Banks are leery of loaning money to construction company ESOPs. They are aware just how vulnerable construction companies are to the vagaries of the economy and other profit costs. They may require that the owner personally guarantee the loan until the ESOP pays it off. Until then, his investments can be taken by the bank if the ESOP defaults.

To summarize: Investment in a construction company is necessary. It's necessary to create a strong and sustainable company. It is necessary if you wish to create a salable company. There are buyers for construction companies. There are a number of ways new owners can purchase a company, from paying cash on the barrelhead to ESOPs. A successful sale could raise enough money to help the owner of a construction company arrive at financial independence.

But know this: Selling a construction company, particularly a micro or small company, is hard. The sale can backfire on the owner unless they get cash up front. A sale is not likely to be as lucrative as the owners imagine.

Victoria Downing, the owner of Remodeler's Advantage (RA), an education and consulting firm that has had many hundreds of clients, says that in her two decades with RA she has rarely seen a company sold successfully. The Winanses' success is the exception, not the rule. Many owners, says Downing, imagine they are going to easily sell their companies and forever after be free of financial worries. That, she says, is "a fantasy." In fact, when she lays out the amount of work they will have to do to actually make their company salable, they tend to shelve their dream.

For a construction company to have a decent chance of being salable, the owner must build a management team. The company should not be a "hub-and-spoke" operation, i.e., one with its owner at the center and entirely responsible for sales, estimating, and basic business decisions. If it is hub-and-spoke, the pool of buyers will be limited to those who can step into, or put a manager into, the owner's shoes.

Such buyers may exist. But ask yourself, would I be willing to be one? Would it be wise to go into debt in order to take over sales, estimating, and all other management of a company someone else has built? Would I not be better off building my own company, one designed to fit me, not a previous owner?

Along with a management team, the owner of a construction company who wants to successfully put it up for sale must have established efficient systems and procedures for handling all work, down to the details. One company whose owner has considered selling even has a protocol for answering the phone. It is answered after two rings, never later, never sooner. That, says the owner, tells callers "we're not desperate for your project, but we are here if you need us."

The salable company is well established and has a strong reputation. Customer satisfaction rates are high. Satisfied customers refer new customers. A well-developed marketing program attracts other customers. The company is not entirely dependent on just a few customers. It has many customers.

Jason Thomas of RainCatcher, a brokerage with experience in selling small construction companies, emphasizes that a company is more attractive to buyers if it has a reliable and recurrent revenue stream. Consequently, mechanical contractors who provide clients with regular maintenance are more marketable and command a higher price than remodeling and general contractors that largely do one-offs. Likewise, for security companies that maintain as well as install systems. They sell for nearly three times as much as companies that only do installations but do not monitor and maintain their systems.

Critically, the salable company has strong financials. It is not working under the cloud of a lawsuit or other liabilities. It has a strong balance sheet and ideally, like Wally Staples's company, is free of debt. Income and expenses are accurately and transparently recorded.

Its books are clean. The books match up to the tax returns. If the owner has been keeping double books, one for minimizing income for taxes and insurance premiums, the other for impressing potential buyers, they have jeopardized their chances of selling their company (along with making themselves vulnerable to criminal charges for fraud).

An owner's chance of selling their company can be dependent on lucky timing. Paul and Nina Winans discovered that. When they put their company up for sale, the construction business was booming. It looked financially attractive. The Winanses found a buyer. Shortly after they sold, construction went from boom to bust. The financial crisis of 2007 had commenced. It snuffed out construction businesses nationwide, including Winans Construction. Under its new owner, the company went bankrupt.

Had the Winanses delayed putting their company up for sale for another year, it may well not have sold, at least not for an acceptable price. Even at the best of times, there seem to be many more would-be sellers of construction companies than buyers. Buyers disappear when construction companies are struggling to survive. Brokers tell construction company owners, "If business is good and you want to sell, don't delay. If you wait and recession strikes, your chances for a sale may evaporate."

Given all the challenges of selling a construction company, one has to ask: Why aim for a sale in the first place, especially if you have a strong hub-and-spoke company? Consider the challenges and costs: To convert your company into a salable business, you will have to greatly enlarge overhead as you hire people to handle management functions that you have been handling yourself. To generate sufficient income to cover the overhead, you must grow volume. The increase in overhead can squeeze profit percentage. During downturns in the economy, it almost surely will.

At the same time, the greater volume increases the risk of profit costs. More work equals more chance of errors in bidding or estimating, of building failures, and of conflict with customers. A salesman, too eager to make sales, promises clients too much for too little. An estimator, distracted by personal problems, overlooks major items in a project and woefully underprices it. A few such mistakes can put a company under.

All in all, you may find that you have created a toxic brew: Narrower profit margins coupled with increased risk. Overall, a sharply lower margin of safety.

Some construction pros, like Steve Nicholls, who built his eighty-person company before selling it to his employees, relish the challenge of building up volume. They justifiably take pride in creating a company that will continue to provide their employees with a good living after they have left it. They have tried to do something hard. They have succeeded.

Let's celebrate their achievement. But let's also not underestimate its costs. Nicholls himself candidly speaks of the enormous stress he endured when struggling to survive hard times. And Bo Burlingham, author of *Small Giants,* observes, "When you are bent on maximizing growth you have very little freedom. You are a slave to the business. While the experience can be exhilarating, it leaves little time for anything else."

Why go that way, Gino Wickman wonders in his book *Traction.* Having a big company is "not all it's cracked up to be," he says. Wickman asks whether you would rather have a $10 million company with a 2 percent profit margin or a $1 million company with a 20 percent profit margin? After all, they both generate profits of $200,000 a year.

That brings us back to our original question: If you have a strong hub-and-spoke operation, will you really enjoy a net benefit if you take on the burdens of growth and risk that will likely be necessary to make your business salable? The answer is for each construction pro to determine for themselves. My answer for myself was, "No." I think that for most of us who are general contractors or even specialty contractors the answer is likely no. Few of us will enjoy enough benefit from the growth necessary to make a company salable to offset the costs.

You may think differently. If you are leaning toward "Yes, I want to build a big company and then sell it," then before making up your mind for good you ought to consider one more question: How much money can one reasonably expect to receive from the sale of a construction company?

The answer is somewhat elusive, but one thing is clear. The company's sales value is derived not so much from its volume of work or total revenue as from its profits. What buyers, at least financially literate buyers, are concerned with when they make an investment in a construction company is the future cash flows their investment will bring them.

They are, as we described in a previous chapter, discounting future cash flows back to present value (PV). And PV is the price they would be willing to pay for the business. "I am willing to pay x dollars for this company," a buyer says to themselves, "because I think it will generate y dollars of profit annually in the future."

To determine present value and set a selling price for a company, a multiplier is applied to its annual profit. The multiplier may be 1, 2, or 3, or more, and the profit is multiplied by that figure. If a company's annual profit is $300,000 and a multiplier of 2 is appropriate, then the company's present value and selling price would be $600,000 (300,000 × 2 = 600,000). If the appropriate multiplier is 3, then the selling price would be $900,000 (300,000 × 3 = 900,000).

When we go in search of multipliers that can be applied to a construction company's profit to determine its price, we encounter a range of possibilities. They come from brokers who specialize in selling small businesses.

The most optimistic broker I have encountered suggests the following multipliers: For painting, drywall or insulation contractors, 3 to 4. For remodelers, 3 to 4.5. For general contractors, 3 to 5. For HVAC, plumbing, or mechanical contractors, 3.5 to 5.5. In other words, if you own a saleable general contracting firm with half million dollars annual profit, you might, according to the optimistic brokers, get $1.5 to $2.5 million for it.

Two less optimistic brokers agree that for construction companies in general a multiplier of 2 or 3 is realistic. Having seen half a dozen sales of construction companies, I am dubious about even those multipliers. I suspect they may be high and that multipliers below 2 could be more realistic.

A third broker adds an even more sobering note: The multiplier can drop as low as 1 for construction companies. (Yes, 1 × profit, so that a company that earns $300,000 profit annually would sell for just $300,000.) Further, brokers warn that a high percentage of construction companies that get listed never sell at all. And that even if they do sell, it is not for cash on the barrelhead. Rather, payment is delivered over several years – if the company stays in business. To add insult to injury, the broker will take a commission, typically around 10 percent of the selling price, whether the owner gets fully paid or not.

If you are a construction pro interested in achieving financial freedom, you may have better options than devoting decades and much of the cash from your investment bucket to creating a salable company. You can instead build a compact, lean, and efficient company, a classy hub-and-spoke operation beloved by its customers. Even during weak economies, the company can likely pay its bills, including your pay for management, and scrounge up enough work to keep its crew busy. During strong economies it pays you, provides good work to employees, allows you to share profit with them, and pumps cash into your investment bucket.

You pour enough of that cash back into your company to keep it strong. But you go no further. You realize that if you did, you would thereby be investing in one of the most financially anemic of all business sectors – construction! You choose instead to make investments that tend to produce better financial results – like those we will be discussing in the coming chapters.

Such investments can be made in such a way that they pump out cash even as they burden you with little management responsibility and their market value increases. A portfolio of such investments can free you of the necessity to work for income. Acquire them, and you will have financial freedom.

As a bonus, you still own your construction company. You may elect to roll it up for a time to pursue other interests. But you will have the option of hanging out your shingle again and taking on projects down the road. That, in fact, is what I did after I had arrived at financial independence. I closed my company. I moved into new ventures. But now and then I would unfurl David Gerstel/Builder and take on a building project. Other builders I know do something similar. They mark off lengthy periods on their calendars for travel or other activity between projects, then go back at it.

I have figured that had I wanted to go back to building full time, in just a couple of years during a strong economy, I could have made as much money as I would have netted from a sale of my company. You may want to crunch some numbers and see if that is the case for you. It may well be.

Judith Miller, the veteran construction industry financial analyst and business coach who has observed hundreds of construction companies, says she sees well-run hub-and-spoke operations providing their owners $600,000 a year in pay and profit. From what I have seen and learned, they would be fortunate to sell their companies for even twice that amount. And that would be even after taking the risks and making the investment of time and spirit to enlarge it.

The numbers suggest that selling a small construction company is a dubious proposition financially. Of course, owners who decide to sell are often concerned about more than financial outcomes. They are also concerned about their employees, the people with whom they have worked shoulder to shoulder for years. And they are concerned about their "legacy." They've built a business. They like seeing its name, which very well may be their own name, on their trucks and on jobsite signs around town. They don't want to see their legacy fade away.

One solution is the setting up of an ESOP, the employee stock ownership plan described earlier in this chapter. But for smaller companies an ESOP may not be an option. No one in the business can step into the owner's role. Sale via a broker may also not be appealing. If the owner lists the company with a broker and the business does sell, then the owner is putting the lives of the employees in the hands of a stranger.

Fortunately, there is another way of taking care of your employees as you move out of your company. That's the option I chose. I rolled the company up gradually, supporting my employees in their move to the next stage of their lives.

Some of my employees have started and are successfully running their own construction companies. One has become the "indispensable" project manager for a builder to whom I recommended him. Others went to work for public agencies that regulate construction work. I am proud of them all. They contributed enormously to the success of David Gerstel/Builder. Their experience in our company is a part of the foundation of their success and enables the contributions they continue to make. That is legacy enough for me.

Investing in Real Estate I: Possibilities

After learning to make a profit and to store up capital, investing is a next useful move for a construction pro seeking financial freedom. Investing in real estate is a natural direction to take. It beckons to construction pros as water does to ducks.

Real estate investing is basically about three things: Purchasing land and building new structures on it. Purchasing land with existing structures and renovating them. Purchasing land with existing structures and maintaining and operating them. (Buying land with or without structures and doing nothing with it in the hope of reselling at a higher price, is not investing. It's just speculating.)

Real estate investing is a pond we know how to swim in. We know buildings. We know how to construct, improve, and maintain them. We know how to do that cost-effectively. As one builder who invests in real estate puts it, we can build for ourselves at wholesale prices.

The house that I call the 19th Street House and that I wrote about in my book *Crafting the Considerate House* serves as an example. I engineered all structural components of the house to maximize performance while minimizing cost. Unfettered by an architect's or owner's specifications and acting as designer, I used salvaged material and shopped hard, finding good materials available at clearance sale prices. The result: I built the 19th Street house for out-of-pocket costs of construction roughly *one third* of retail, i.e., the price that established builders were at the time charging their customers for residential work of similar quality.

At 19th Street, I was building a new house. But the same financial edge exists for renovation. A capable builder can improve a property for a fraction of the dollars the work would cost an owner who must hire contractors to do it.

Construction pros enjoy another advantage in real estate investment. When they work on a property, whether designing or project managing or working with their tools, they are getting paid. They are, however, not getting paid with a check from which taxes are deducted. They are getting paid in the form of the value their work adds to their property.

In other words, as a construction pro investing your time and skill in real estate, you get paid in untaxed dollars. Since you are not getting a paycheck, all of your "pay" goes directly to work as an investment without first being reduced by taxes. Over time, that added value, i.e., equity, that you literally build into your property can compound. You are then building wealth free of taxation until you sell the property.

I want to emphasize that here in this discussion of real estate investing, I am not talking about "house flipping," namely buying a house, improving it, and then putting it right back on the market in hope of a quick profit. House flipping is a variant of spec building, of development. The only difference is that you are starting with a lot and a building rather than an empty lot.

By investing, I mean acquiring land, building on it or renovating buildings that are already on it, and maintaining and renting the property in order to produce the cash flow.

If you decide to invest in real estate, you will have a lot of company. People from all walks of life are out there trying to make their fortune by buying properties.

As a capable construction pro, you enjoy an advantage in the investment property hunt. You are a skilled estimator. You will be able to reliably project the costs of any necessary construction at a property you are considering for purchase. You will not make the mistake of buying a property at too high a price because you woefully underestimated those costs. You will not be scared off by work that you can readily do but that might intimidate amateurs.

Once you have purchased a property, your skills as a construction pro will advantage you again. Unlike investors from outside our profession, you will be able to competently accomplish whatever construction needs to be done. The run-of-the mill real estate investor has a problem there. Tune into the podcasts that cater to real estate investors. You will hear their constant lament. It's voiced by both hosts and guests. "The one thing we investors struggle with most," says one host, "is the general contractor. That is the biggest thorn in my side."

I personally know many capable and reliable builders. I suspect the investors' problems arise from their trying to get things done on the cheap. They want a Ford F-150 Lightning right out of the showroom for the price of a beat-up VW van. Whatever the case, you won't have their problem. You have a capable contractor: yourself.

Once you have completed construction at your property and are ready to choose a tenant, your experience will again prove valuable. Your experience at qualifying clients for your construction services readies you for the work of qualifying tenants. You know that signing a contract with a bad client can make for a prolonged miserable experience. You will realize that prospective tenants must be screened as carefully as potential clients for construction projects.

Cautionary tale: The owner of a house across the street from my project on 19th Street did not take the trouble to select new tenants for his property with care. He did not check their credit rating or talk to past landlords. He did not learn about their employment history or history of encounters with the law.

He just chatted for half an hour with a man and woman who asked about renting his place. The friendly old couple would be lovely tenants, he concluded. He signed a lease with them.

The couple turned out to be the heads of a family of criminals, expert at shaking down landlords. A year after they moved into his place, he had to pay them a $5,000 bribe to move out. In the meanwhile, they had paid no rent for many months. To justify their nonpayment, they claimed one defect in the house after another. When they could not come up with an existing defect, they created one, such as clogging the sewer line so badly it had to be replaced at a cost of thousands of dollars.

With conscientious management, real estate investment can bring substantial rewards. The rewards are both financial and psychological. You can begin to create or even secure your financial freedom with a small number of properties.

One construction pro and his wife bought land in a rural area for cash. For a few thousand dollars they installed a used mobile home on the land and spruced it up. They lived in the mobile while they accumulated additional capital and then built a new home without taking out a loan. At a young age, with a home owned free and clear and a rental (the mobile), they had made a good start down the road to financial independence.

Another pro stored up investment capital, bought an urban lot, then spent a year leading a crew in the construction of an apartment building. The rents from that one building provided more income than he needed to live on.

If you do elect to invest in real estate and dive into the numerous books and podcasts about the enterprise, you will often encounter this advice: "Don't overimprove. Don't put more into your property than is justified by its location."

The advice might be valid for the ordinary investor who must pay market prices for construction. To get an adequate return on their investment, they need to be restrained with improvements. A construction pro is not similarly confined. Given a feeling for design and detail plus an ability to utilize material and labor effectively, a construction pro can "overimprove" for nominal additional cost.

That is what I did at my 19th Street House. It is located in a town and neighborhood of workforce housing inhabited by folks with modest incomes. As possibly the best-built single-family house in the town, it is way "overimproved" for its location. The wall framing is not green 2x4 lumber but kiln-dried and Forest Stewardship Council Certified (FSC) 2x6. Flooring is not linoleum or rental-grade carpeting but tile and wood. Window jambs are not wrapped in drywall but trimmed with clear pine. Tubs and surrounds are not plastic but cast iron and tile. Drywall is ⅝ inch, not ½ inch. Cabinetry is built with ¾ inch maple plywood and solid stock, not pressboard. However, with thorough value engineering and other cost controls (all described in the book), I was able to "overimprove" without unduly running up costs.

Overimprovement, if done frugally, pays off financially. When I put the 19th Street house up for rent, prospective tenants exclaimed over the quality. Dozens of people expressed interest in renting the house. I was able to select tenants who proved reliable in every way.

That experience has been typical of the results for my overimprovement strategy. It has worked in a high as well as a lower-income neighborhood. Even during periods of economic recession when the rental market weakens, I have been able to choose from multiple applicants for my houses.

Another real estate investor who capitalizes on overimprovement is described by Gary Eldred in his authoritative book, *Investing in Real Estate* (see "Resources"). The investor's tenants are students. When he decided to invest in student housing, he began by interviewing and surveying students to learn what they needed. Then he set out to create it and provide apartments that met those needs and were superior to apartments offered by his competitors.

He eliminated rodent and pest infestation, remodeled kitchens, renovated heating and plumbing systems so that they functioned reliably, and landscaped and painted. He built a rooftop addition to serve as quiet study space and, for each apartment, a separate and attractively screened storage unit. The result: He attracts good tenants, students attending college to study, not to party. The investor assures himself of a return on his investment by having his tenants sign a contract that requires that they neither smoke nor drink, maintain a B average or better, and make a deposit twice the usual amount.

Good possibilities for return on investment in real estate arise not only from "overimproving" properties but from their ongoing management. You realize the possibilities by operating from the same understanding that supports success in the construction business. You appreciate that you are in a service business and that you must attentively serve the needs of your clients, i.e., your tenants.

You operate with enlightened self-interest. When your tenants call to let you know a repair is necessary, you handle it immediately (just as you immediately take care of callbacks at your construction projects). You contact your tenants regularly to make sure their needs are being met. You hire a gardener to care for the landscaping. Periodically, you inspect your properties. When maintenance is necessary. you employ skilled people to install good materials.

You reject the attitude embodied in the phrase, too often used by real estate investors, "It's just a rental." Yes, your property is a source of income. But you also understand that it is someone's home and that you have accepted the responsibility of providing them with a well-maintained home.

Gary Eldred tells the story of an investor who operates rentals in low-income neighborhoods and embraces that attitude. Their properties, they say, represent them and are a statement about their character. They take care not only of the land and structures within their property line. They go beyond it, even picking up litter along their street and encouraging other owners to follow their example.

They call their practice "magnetizing the neighborhood." They say it pulls in responsible people and drives out bad actors. The neighborhood improves. As a result, the value of their property rises. What goes around comes around.

Investing care in a property – and charging moderate rents rather than the most the market will allow – pays off. Tenants feel welcomed, not squeezed for maximum financial gain by the property owner. They tend to stay on. Why leave? They are getting a good place at a fair price and have a relationship with an owner they can trust. They are not likely to do better. The low turnover is an owner's financial reward for their efforts to serve their tenants. Vacancies cost money and time.

Sometimes the thought, "Tenants are a pain in the neck," does start to trickle through my mind before I can squash the error and replace the thought with "My reliable tenants are invaluable clients." They are valuable in that they pay their rent promptly and take good care of their places. And they are more than valuable. They are good neighbors. Some have become friends.

The potential human connections that go with being a real estate investor are often overlooked amid all the talk about financial gain. Investors brag about the number of "doors" they own, as if the people who lived behind those doors did not matter at all. Likely their renters suffer from that attitude. The investors do also. They are missing out on rewarding relationships.

On the other hand, financial benefits, while they can be substantial, are often overstated. What I call the "Grandma's house effect" sets in. People exclaim, "My grandmother bought her house for $6,000. Now it's worth $256,000!" They overlook the fact that in the sixty years she owned the house, Grandma made many improvements. She remodeled the original bathroom, added another, and built an expanded and updated kitchen. She had new plumbing supply and waste and drain and heating systems installed. She invested steadily in maintenance from new roofing to painting.

Also overlooked when Grandma's gains are being celebrated: the impact of inflation on the purchasing power of dollars – i.e., the fact that Grandma's $6,000 investment made sixty years earlier had the purchasing power of $40,000 today. If the improvements are factored in and the adjustment for inflation is made, it may turn out that Grandma made little on her house. The purchasing power of the dollars she received for it may turn out to be only marginally more than the purchasing power of the dollars she spent to buy and improve it.

Not credible, you say? Learn then what Robert Shiller, an economist who won the Nobel prize, has discovered. He and his associates extensively researched changes in housing prices in the United States across a period of 116 years. By factoring in improvements made between purchases and sales, they came to a realistic view of the rate of change. Adjusting for inflation, they concluded the *real* average rate of growth in housing prices over the 116 years was 0.4 percent. Yes, just four tenths of one percent annually in inflation adjusted dollars.

Shiller adds additional cautionary notes: Housing prices don't always go up. Between 1890 and 1950, except for a brief period of upward tilt, housing prices actually dropped steadily. Almost all the increase in housing prices over the century preceding the publication of Shiller's book in 2005 occurred in two narrow time slots, one right after WWII and a second in the late 1990s. During the time I have spent writing this book, housing prices have climbed steeply in some parts of the country and in some neighborhoods. In others they have sagged.

You can get lucky and invest in a real estate market destined for an extended boom. A friend of mine has been fortunate to invest in Austin, Texas, where property prices have been climbing rapidly for years. I have been fortunate to invest in the San Francisco Bay Area, which has enjoyed an even longer surge (though one punctuated by periods when real estate prices crumbled and houses lost half or more of their market value). Had I lived and worked elsewhere, the rise in the value of my properties might have been more modest or nonexistent.

The fate of a market often seems obvious after it has played out. We can fool ourselves into thinking that had we taken a look we would have known what was going to happen ahead of time. That is called "postdiction" or "retroactive clairvoyance," predicting something will take place after it has taken place. Postdiction is easy. Prediction, not so easy.

It is not possible to know in advance when or whether a real estate market is going to go down or up. Could investors in Detroit have anticipated that the price of a house and lot in some neighborhoods would drop to $150? Could someone renting out apartments in the slums of Brooklyn decades ago have forecast that their shabby properties would become multi-million-dollar condos?

Could a builder who bought and renovated two Victorian houses in Kansas City have anticipated his results? During the Great Recession of 2007 the value of his properties collapsed. More than a decade later they remained underwater.

Much of the information we are fed about real estate investing has an evangelical quality. Come to God and grow rich is the pitch. Don't be afraid. Just jump in. The water is warm. Little is said about the risks and downsides. And what is said tends to be muted and only vaguely cautionary.

On a popular real estate podcast, I hear younger people celebrating their investment gains. A few of them are wise enough to appreciate how lucky they have been. Many invested during that period after the financial crises of 2007 when property prices had collapsed. Subsequently, they enjoyed the rebound in prices that followed as the supply of housing in the United States was outstripped by demand.

Too often the guests on the podcast seem to attribute their success to entrepreneurial daring and smarts. They are like the builders I wrote about in an earlier chapter, who chalk up their success during a boom to exceptional business acumen. Neither the investors nor the builders speak much of having also been lucky.

I have yet to hear a guest on the investor podcasts who candidly reported setbacks such as that experienced by the Kansas City builder. And I have not heard a peep from any of the guests who, like an entrepreneurial friend of mine, got wiped out in the 2007 financial crises. When he saw opportunity in real estate beginning around 2001, he plunged in. Taking on huge amounts of mortgage debt, he rapidly bought homes during the time when speculation in housing was replacing the stock market speculation of the late twentieth century. Quickly, he became a millionaire many times over and went shopping for a vacation chalet in France.

I urged him to sell his rentals: "We are in a bubble, like the stock market bubble that collapsed a few years ago. Get out now. Take your winnings and diversify your investments. You will be fixed for life."

He did not sell. "Real estate never loses value," he told me. "The government can't allow it to. The whole economy would collapse."

Housing prices did collapse. They fell by about a third on average nationally and 70 percent or more in the neighborhoods where my friend was investing. The housing bust did devastate the entire U.S. economy despite government efforts to shore it up.

My friend never got his chalet. His millions of dollars in equity in his houses dissolved. Tenants who had lost their jobs could not pay their rent. He could not make his mortgage payments. His bank foreclosed on all his investment properties. Then it took his home. Last I heard, he had moved to a country in Latin America where living was cheap in hope of being able to support his family on the modest savings salvaged from his real estate disaster.

In sum: Real estate investment does hold promise for the capable construction pro seeking financial freedom. We have acquired skills that are valuable in property acquisition and management from our work running our construction businesses. We enjoy advantages both in the construction and the operation of properties.

We need, however, to be realistic about the possibilities. One seasoned real estate investor warns us to not fall prey to "survivor bias." In other words, he cautions, don't heed the stories only of those who have invested and prospered. Learn also from the tales of those who have not.

Good possibilities await. Realizing them requires focus, skill, good judgment, and effort, along with a bit of luck. Just as with the management of our construction companies, to realize the possibilities in real estate investment, we have to bear down and get things done right.

Investing in Real Estate II: Execution

Making a real estate investment involves four processes: Searching for a property. Qualifying it for an offer. Purchasing the property. Operating it.

The search alone can require persistence. During down markets, properties can sometimes be had for less than the cost of replacing whatever structure sits on the lot. You get the structure at a discount and get the lot free. However, a decade and more can pass between such markets. There have been significant downturns in the U.S. real estate market in (roughly) 1975, 1985, 1990, and 2010. There may be another one around the corner as I write this book in 2020. We'll see.

During stronger markets, finding a property at a price that allows for cash flow and a good chance of appreciation is likely to be time-consuming. By one knowledgeable estimate, a real estate investor will – to obtain just one property – typically spend about 20 hours scanning ads for possibilities. Then spend 200 more hours checking them out more closely. And finally, put in an additional 100 hours making offers, inspecting properties inside and out, and closing a deal. All told that adds up to two months full-time work.

A search for prospects can be broad in scope or narrow. You can search all across your state or region and even nationally. A consulting client of mine on the West Coast recently decided to invest in a town in Florida. Alternatively, you can settle on a specific neighborhood where you think you will be comfortable operating as a property owner. I've never invested in real estate more than twelve minutes from my office.

Whatever your choice, once you have chosen a neighborhood for consideration, you need to learn about it – not only as a construction pro interested in buildings but from the perspective of an investor gauging potential financial outcomes. Talk to local realtors, residents, and shopkeepers. Learn about the availability of public transportation, the reputation of the local schools, and the competence of local government. Determine whether the neighborhood is improving or declining and whether there is demand for rentals.

If the neighborhood looks good in overview, zoom in for a closer look. Are the streets in good condition? Are they littered or clean? Are people taking care of their yards and the exteriors of their buildings? Are too many storefronts closed up or are local businesses doing okay?

Once you have settled on a neighborhood, begin looking for a specific property to purchase. Possibly you will find a realtor who will bring likely candidates to you. But realtors are often investors inclined to pick off the most promising properties for themselves.

If realtors are not serving you, try using their tactics for finding properties. Let residents of the neighborhood that interests you know that you are looking for a property to purchase. Send postcards to property owners. Distribute flyers or door hangers. Keep at it. You may turn up a good possibility. My own best real estate investment resulted from my staying in touch with the owner for several years.

Alternatively, you can go shopping among properties that have been taken by a bank, private lender, or government agency – i.e. foreclosures and real estate owned properties (REOs), foreclosed properties a lender has been unable to sell at auction. You may be able to pick up a property for a bargain price. During down markets, foreclosures and REOs may be especially abundant. One caution though: If you elect to go after them, first educate yourself about the challenges and hazards. The excellent book on real estate investing by Gary Eldred that I describe in "Resources" will get you started.

Other cautions: Don't buy a property because of a single feature without regard for the bigger picture. In particular, avoid the rookie mistake Max made. It's an error that we construction pros, with our romantic attachment to well-crafted buildings, can be susceptible to. It's buying a property simply because you are drawn to the building, as Max did when he bought an architecturally appealing but dilapidated duplex in a rough neighborhood and found that he could not successfully manage it.

When you are making your first property purchase, don't rush in. You may be eager to get underway as a real estate investor. But don't let emotion blind you to the costs of building or renovating the property. That's a mistake akin to fooling yourself about the costs of construction for a client's project because you want the job too much. If someone else wants to fool themselves and overpay for a "fixer-upper" or "contractor special" (as, unfortunately, amateurs often do), step aside and let them.

Likewise, do not fool yourself about operating costs. You know buildings. You know that every single system in a building from the foundation to the paint is liable to decline and eventual failure. Use that knowledge to project a realistic maintenance budget.

As you tote up the expenses of operating the place, allow for the value of your management as we stressed earlier. Make a realistic projection of rents – one that includes a vacancy factor. With those calculations completed, you will be able to figure the potential net income from the property you are considering. Then you will be able to determine what you can prudently offer for it.

If you are a construction pro looking to secure financial freedom, then cash flow, i.e., net income after all expenses, must be a top priority during your property search. If a property does not produce a flow of cash from the outset, then you have made a predominantly speculative investment. You are counting on achieving a return due to a rise in the market price of the property that may or may not occur.

When evaluating a property with a focus on cash flow, experienced investors look at "capitalization rate," or "cap rate" for short. Cap rate is determined by dividing projected net income from a property by its market price. If the net income for a property is projected as $10,000 annually and the market price is $80,000, then the cap rate is 12.5 percent ($10,000 \div 80,000 = 10 \div 80 = 1 \div 8 = 12.5$ percent).

After they have purchased a property, real estate investors measure the actual financial performance of the property in terms of "cash-on-cash" return. For example, in the case described in the preceding paragraph, assume the investor put $80,000 of their own money into the property. Because of unforeseen costs, they ended up with a net income of only $8,000 rather than the projected $10,000. In that case, they are enjoying a cash-on-cash return of 10 percent ($8,000 \div 80,000 = 8 \div 80 = 1 \div 10 = 10\%$), as opposed to the 12.5 percent they had projected when calculating cap rate.

Experienced real estate investors use yet another metric to evaluate financial performance, namely "internal rate of return (IRR)." IRR, as used for real estate investment purposes, takes into account two other financial benefits in addition to cash-on-cash return: Possible appreciation in the market value of a property. And possible tax benefits (such as write-offs for depreciation). For example, if the cash-on-cash return is 10 percent, appreciation is projected at 3 percent annually, and tax benefits at another 2 percent of the investment, then the IRR is 15 percent ($10 + 3 + 2 = 15$).

All three measures – cap rate, cash-on-cash, IRR – are to a degree guesswork. With cap rate calculations you are making assumptions about future income. With IRR you are hoping in addition for appreciation which may or may not materialize. Even with cash-on-cash calculations you may be assuming and hoping that present income flows will continue in the future. That, too, may or may not happen.

You've probably noticed that cap rate and cash-on-cash calculations have a family resemblance to the present value calcs we discussed in "Deploying Capital." With both, you are trying to assess future financial benefits. A prime difference is that with present value you are comparing the potential earnings to those offered by a benchmark such as a U.S. bond.

With IRR there is no close parallel to present value calcs. Various sources of real estate advice do, however, suggest minimum acceptable IRRs that can serve as benchmarks. One suggests 15 percent across the board. Another suggests 10 percent for a prime property, 15 percent for a distressed property, and 20 percent for new development.

Those guidelines strike me as reasonable, as incorporating adequate margin of safety. Some real estate advisors, however, dismiss hard and fast rules. Cap rate and IRR, they think, should be considered within the overall "context" for a property – i.e., with respect to possibilities that are not reflected in the standard formulations.

For a construction pro, context includes the possibilities for developing the property at wholesale prices. I have discussed such possibilities in the previous chapter. I won't belabor the subject here. The bottom line is this: Capable builders can enhance a property with effective and imaginative use of labor and material and do so for significantly lower costs than investors who do not have their skills. Building at wholesale prices, construction pros can reap retail returns on their investment.

That is what I did at the property on 19th Street, also described in the previous chapter. The property originally consisted of a large lot with a two-bedroom bungalow to one side. I split the lot and, putting my skills as a builder to work, renovated the bungalow and sold it. Then I constructed the 19th Street House for a cost roughly equal to the profits from the sale of the bungalow.

At that point, I owned a high quality four-bedroom house with two and a half baths, free and clear. I rented it to reliable tenants for a decade, enjoying strong cash flows, tax shelter, and steady appreciation. Although my ownership of the properties spanned the Great Recession of 2007–2009 and the attendant crash in real estate values, my overall returns were respectable.

I could provide more examples. But the key points are made. Buy with cash flow in mind. Buy with an eye to employing your skills as a construction pro to increase cash flow and the market value of your property.

As you move from purchasing a property to operating it as a rental, your skills as a construction pro will once again give you an edge. The practices that have supported success in your building business will translate to the rental business.

As in construction, you want to offer a superior product at a competitive price. The frugality (i.e., careful use of resources, not stinginess) you have honed as a builder, will enable that. With property operation, as with construction, you can find many opportunities to reduce cost without impairing the services you provide to your clients – who, in the case of rental properties, are your tenants.

A few obvious examples of frugality are low-maintenance but attractive landscaping, low-flow plumbing devices, and energy-efficient lighting.

Less obvious: Trimming away low-benefit/high-cost coverages when purchasing insurance (though only with the guidance of an insurance broker who specializes in real estate insurance). Also, hiring pros skilled at their trade for repairs and maintenance; avoiding handymen.

Handymen are slow. They are costly. Their hourly rates may be half that of a pro, but when they take three times as long to do a task, they are then 50 percent more expensive (I leave the math to you). Worse, they make serious mistakes. Their work fails and has to be done over. I looked for a competent handyman for years. I never found one. Now

I hire experienced plumbers, electricians, painters, and other pros for maintenance work I don't want to do myself.

As with rigorous overhead management for your construction company, by trimming away costs in the operation of a rental property you increase the potential for cash flow. You thereby increase the value of your property. No matter how it is calculated, the value of rental property is in good measure determined by cash flow. By increasing cash flow via cost control, so long as it does not compromise the quality of your property, you push up value.

Just as you do with your construction company, you must put protections around your rental business. The single most important protection is exercising care in the selection of the people you get involved with. Like a bad client for a construction project, the wrong tenant can make your life miserable and cost you heavily in money and time. Case in point: The criminals, described in the previous chapter, who occupied the house across from my 19th Street project.

A good tenant is a person whom it is a pleasure to do business with. To select good tenants, develop a qualification procedure as thorough as the one you have created for clients for construction work. Learn everything you can about a prospective tenant. Learn about their credit history. Learn about their employment history. Talk to owners from whom they have previously rented, ending each conversation with a question: "Would you rent to them again?" If you don't immediately get a sincere "Yes," consider that a flashing yellow caution light. Owners are constrained from saying what they really have to say about bad tenants.

Once you have selected a tenant, invite them to your office for the signing of the contract, your next line of protection as the operator of a rental business. Properly used, a contract sets up a cooperative, not an adversarial relationship. It makes clear your obligations to the tenant and theirs to you. It commits both you and the tenant to honoring those obligations.

A contract can do all that with the use of straightforward and even friendly language. Gary Eldred advises against using "fine print forms written in legal jargon ... with their long lists of authoritarian dos and don'ts." I agree. I have built my contract from the clauses in rental agreements written by attorneys specializing in real estate. But I have translated the jargon into clear English, placed a contents page at the beginning of the contract, and used highlights to make the document friendlier. If you are not comfortable with such a DIY option, you can still hold down costs by finding a contract tailored to the requirements of your state online, purchasing it, then paying an attorney to check it over and suggest modifications.

Ask new tenants to go over the contract carefully. That will take time. A good contract, though friendly in tone, is not short. (Mine is five pages, though of large print with a lot of white space.) Spend the time. Just as in construction, a good contract understood by all who will sign it prevents surprises down the line.

I always ask tenants to let me know if any of the clauses in my contract trouble them and indicate willingness to adjust if possible. No one has ever asked for adjustments other than the guy who pointed out a missing comma and a spelling error and had me make corrections. (That's the kind of meticulous tenant you want! The guy was a reliable tenant who paid with unfailing promptness and took good care of the house I rented to him and his family for years.) If someone asked for a reasonable and fair adjustment, I would happily make it.

Once a tenant has moved in, make sure you fulfill your contractual obligations – and then some! As stressed in the previous chapter, take care of your property. Promptly do repairs. Check in with tenants now and then to see if their house is working properly or needs attention.

If a tenant begins to slip on their obligations, let them know that they need to step up. Tell them once face-to-face and in a friendly fashion. If they do not respond, tell them in writing with no punches pulled. That will probably do the job. Written warnings are powerful. If the tenant still does not respond, hire an eviction expert to help you move them out. Eviction is just like any other repair. You need a pro to do it.

In addition to a thorough contract with carefully qualified tenants, successful operation of a rental business requires several other protections. It requires a distinct set of books. You don't want to comingle your accounts for construction and for rentals. If you do, you will fog your vision of the financial performance of both operations.

Your rental business must have its own capital reserves. Costly building failures, like a water heater splitting open and soaking the flooring, can happen unexpectedly. Prolonged vacancies can develop. Good tenants can become unable to pay rent for a time, as has been the case for many during the COVID-19 pandemic. You can make a mistake and choose a bad tenant. Eviction can become necessary. For all such developments, you need cash in reserve.

Though you want to prune away unnecessary coverage (with the guidance of that carefully selected broker) in the interest of restraining expenses, you do need comprehensive insurance from a good company. Find the good companies by networking with other property owners. Learn which brokers they trust to set them up with a reliable insurance company. Choose one of them. Avoid the lowballing companies.

A client of mine failed to do that. A reservoir above his property overflowed, releasing a river of water that plunged down the steep driveway and through the front entry, flooding and devastating the building. His lowballing insurance company came up with a repair estimate that was one-quarter the amount of the estimates submitted by two respected builders. The client had to go through years of litigation against his insurer in order to get a settlement adequate to cover the cost of repairs.

As a final protection, you may want to enclose your rental property in a separate corporation (or your several rental properties in several separate corporations). Then, if a client sues your construction company, they will be constrained from laying claim to your rental properties.

Likewise, tenants of one property will be constrained from laying claim to other properties in a legal dispute.

We have gone through the fundamentals of real estate investing: Search. Qualify. Purchase. Operate. I'd like to circle back to Purchase. Given my views on debt expressed in earlier chapters, it will not surprise you that I favor investing in real estate without use of debt. For the construction pro, that is possible. If you operate a lean company, you can stockpile capital steadily. Using your capital, you can acquire property without borrowing and then, with your professional skills, improve it at wholesale prices.

As a result, you will own real estate that produces steady cash flow and is free of obligations to lenders. No one will be in a position to seize your property should you hit a rough patch and be unable to make mortgage payments. That's protection.

My views on avoiding debt when investing in real estate are unusual. I must acknowledge that others do make forceful arguments for using leverage, even maximum leverage. Here let's contrast the possible outcomes, benefits, and costs of their approaches and mine by looking at two alternative paths to acquiring real estate.

Suppose on the one hand that you invest $150,000 of the cash from your investment bucket in a single property. You buy it without use of leverage and own it free and clear. You collect $20,000 in rent annually and pay $5,000 for taxes, insurance, maintenance, and other expenses. That leaves you $15,000 net income from the property. That is a 10 percent return on your investment ($15,000 \div 150,000 = 1 \div 10 = 10$ percent).

Suppose on the other hand that you decide to make use of leverage. You invest only $30,000 of your capital, take out a mortgage for $120,000, collect the same $20K for rent, and have expenses, including the mortgage payments, of $12,000. That leaves you with $8,000 income ($20,000 - 12,000 = 8,000$). Your cash-on-cash return on the $30,000 you have invested is then not 10 percent but almost 27 percent ($8,000 \div 30,000 = .267$, which rounds off to 27 percent). Though your cash flow has dropped by almost half, from $15,000 to $8,000, your cash-on-cash return, in percentage terms, almost tripled.

After that first leveraged purchase, you still have $120,000 in your investment bucket (150K – 30K = 120K). You use it to buy four more properties, investing $30,000 of your cash and taking out a loan for $120,000 for each of them. Now you have five properties, all of them (assuming the same income and expenses as for the first property) with a cash-on-cash return of 27 percent. Wow! You are now making 27 percent on your whole $150,000. That's over $40,000 a year.

And there's more good news yet to come: Assume your five properties appreciate at an average annual rate of 3 percent, or $22,500 the first year and, due to compounding, more in subsequent years. (I will leave the math to you). With only one property instead of five you would enjoy only one fifth as much annual appreciation.

That, in a nutshell, is the argument for using leverage.

The arguments against leverage are much simpler. Appreciation is not guaranteed. Properties can lose rather than gain value. Rents can decline so much or vacancies become so frequent for a time that rather than producing cash flow, a leveraged property instead burns through cash.

Worse, you can lose properties to the mortgage holder, even after years of paying down your mortgages. You hit a period of severe economic breakdown. Your construction business is providing you with barely enough to live on. Your tenants have lost their jobs and cannot pay rent. You, as a result, cannot pay your mortgages. The mortgage holder then takes "your" property that, as it turns out, was not really yours after all.

Think that simply will not, cannot, and does not happen? I have seen foreclosures accelerate twice in just the last decade. It was around 2010 that my friend who was forced to move to Latin America to feed his family lost his leveraged rental properties (something like thirty of them if memory serves) to foreclosure. As I write this book ten years later, property owners all over the U.S. are unable to collect rent from tenants whose lives have been devasted by the COVID-19 pandemic. An avalanche of foreclosures threatens again.

As a construction pro, you do not need leverage to acquire multiple properties. With one acquired and providing cash flow to supplement the profits you earn in construction, you will build up capital that much more rapidly. You will be able to acquire another property free and clear. And now, with cash flows from two properties, you will soon be ready to acquire the third property free of debt. And so on.

You may recall Wally Staples, the builder I introduced you to in an earlier chapter who operates a debt free construction company. Staples has created just such a progression for himself. Now, just midway through his career, he owns, in addition to his office and shop, six rental houses that he either built or renovated.

Early in his real estate investment career Staples did take out a few low-interest equity loans. But since then he has acquired his rental properties without use of borrowed money. "Rentals fit nicely with my expertise," he says, "but I do not want to owe anyone anything."

If your goal is financial freedom, you may not wish to have many properties. Real estate requires management. The work of management will tie you down. It will impair your freedom. I once raised the subject with a friend who owns multiple properties. She laughed at the idea that owning real estate conveyed freedom and listed the problems she had taken care of in just the preceding week: Failed water heater. Clogged sewer line that had to be replaced. Advertising for new tenants. Picking up after a co-investor who was having mental problems and had dropped the ball on several issues.

Yes, you can hire a manager to take the load off. Trouble is, you may not be able to find a good property manager. John Reed, a real estate author and advisor, says you won't. "They almost all neglect the properties and take kickbacks," he claims angrily.

I don't know about "all," but I do regularly hear warnings about hiring real estate managers. If your manager is not on top of things, you can suffer. One construction pro hired a manager for his rental house in a desirable neighborhood. Four years later a tenant brought in by the manager moved out. When the owner went to take a look at his property, he discovered that damage done by the tenant would cost tens of thousands of dollars to repair.

None of that is to say that real estate is not a good investment for the construction pro. For all the reasons we have discussed, and despite all the challenges, it is a natural, advantageous, and potentially satisfying form of investment. If you invest only in real estate, however, you will have all your investment eggs in one basket. That is especially the case if you invest only in the area in which you live.

If you invest elsewhere, you lose the potential for satisfying, neighborly relationships and assume the hassle or risk of absentee landlordship. You will either have to regularly commute long distances or you will have to take your chances with a property manager.

To enhance freedom and manage risk, you may want to diversify your investments. There is a big world of other investments out there. Unlike real estate, some can be virtually put on automatic pilot. With a portfolio of such investments you can arrive at nearly complete financial freedom.

Investing in the World Economy

After his early debacle with real estate, Max, as you may recall, had gone into learning mode. When he was satisfied that he had a grip on the search-qualify-purchase-operate cycle of real estate investment, he ventured back into the marketplace. Briefly he looked at properties advertised as "fixer uppers" and "contractor specials." It looked to Max like the amateurs who were buying them were naïve about the renovation costs they were facing. The fixers were selling for much more than what Max figured to be their actual present value.

Max turned to a different strategy, one that allowed him to capitalize on his skills as a construction pro. He filled his investment capital bucket, bought a lot, filled the bucket again, built a new house on the lot, then reset and repeated. The strategy worked as well for Max as it would for Wally Staples years later in Maine.

With three houses occupied by reliable tenants, Max had reached the point where he no longer had to work for financial reasons, other than to manage the properties. He did not close his construction company. He enjoyed running it. He realized his investments were not yet sufficient to see him through really hard times. Max had read the history of American capitalism. He understood not only what a powerful economic engine it was, but also that America was prone to periods of economic recession, even depression, and steep inflation.

Max hesitated, however, to build more rental properties. He'd found there was a downside to owning other people's homes. Maintenance calls could come at any time. When tenants moved out, selecting new ones consumed many hours and tied Max down for days. Sometimes Max would show a house to dozens of prospective tenants before finding folks he was confident he wanted to do business with.

Max began to look farther afield for investment possibilities, asking friends with their own businesses for ideas. One extolled his car washes. Another touted storage facilities. A third laundromats. A fourth parking lots. Max looked into all four possibilities. The financials were appealing. But such businesses would need managers. Good managers, Max knew, were hard to come by. A bad one could do damage in a hurry, forcing you to step in and run the business yourself. Max did not want to spend one day of his life running a car wash, storage facility, parking lot, or laundromat.

Max kept exploring. He saw that there were investment possibilities far beyond owning rental properties or small businesses in his own town. His first investment further afield was another disaster. Acting on a hot tip from a client he respected for his analytical ability, Max invested in a technology start-up that promptly went bankrupt.

"Sometimes you win, sometimes you learn," Max again reminded himself. He felt relieved that he had put only a small amount of capital into the start-up. He decided to focus on investing in established companies rather than in brand new enterprises that someone was convincingly touting as "the next big thing" and that *might* amount to something substantial someday. There were, Max observed, a lot of long-lived companies in America and spread across the world that made good products and seemed to be doing just fine. He could invest in them by buying their stocks and bonds.

For guidance, Max relied primarily on Graham and Bogle. He did seek out other financial sages, men and women who had long-term records of success in investing. After all, Graham and Bogle had both done their work during the late twentieth century and had since passed away. One would think that some other sage would have come along in the meanwhile.

As far as Max could see, none had. The men and women who followed Graham and Bogle had not significantly added to, altered, or departed from the wisdom or practices of the two men. Warren Buffett, the most respected investor of the late twentieth and early twenty-first centuries, continued to revere Graham as *his* mentor. And he advised that by and large investors, including his own family, should put their money *not* into his company, Berkshire Hathaway, but into mutual funds offered by Vanguard, the company John Bogle had founded!

From Graham and Bogle, Max came to understand that the market for stocks and bonds was more than a "gambling casino," as another construction pro warned him. Yes, people who fancied themselves to be investors but were really just speculators treated it as if it were a casino.

The way Max saw matters, when you purchased a stock, what you were actually doing was buying a share of ownership in a company, not a poker chip. When you purchased a bond issued by a company, or a government agency, you were in effect loaning money to that company or agency. As a stockholder, you shared in the earnings of your company. As the holder of a bond, you were entitled to interest and eventual repayment of your loan.

Once he had come to that understanding, Max felt investment in stocks and bonds was his best next step. He had realized that with three rental houses plus his own home in a single metro area he had all his eggs in one basket. And the basket itself was liable to getting shredded. His metro area was prosperous. But like many others, it was heavily dependent on a single primary industry. That industry conceivably could relocate as the car industry had relocated from Detroit, devastating real estate values in Max's area.

Ownership of the stocks and bonds of a wide range of companies would solve his problems, Max decided. Investing in them gave him a way to put his capital to work beyond owning more local real estate or buying small local businesses. With headquarters and operations in far-flung places and doing business all over the planet, the companies would provide investment diversity far beyond what Max could achieve locally.

On top of that, Max thought, stock and bond ownership relieved him of the confining management responsibility that came with real estate ownership. Yes, he would need to keep an eye on a stock and bond portfolio. But it would not burden him with early a.m. emails demanding his immediate attention to a running toilet, failed water heater, mouse invasion, or turkeys trampling around on a roof.

Max began his foray into stocks and bonds by researching individual companies to invest in. He soon saw, however, that astute stock and bond selection requires steady reading of business journals and delving into the financial statements, footnotes and all, of the individual companies. By attending courses in financial analysis at a local college, Max did learn how to select financially sound and promising companies. He liked the learning. But he did not like the work as a full-time gig.

Max saw that if he continued to seek individual companies for investment the work would consume him. He would have to not only select companies for investment but keep an eye on them to determine whether he should or should not stick with them. That job would be as confining as owning rentals.

Max began looking for a broker to select his stocks and bonds for him. His first talk with man from a major brokerage was not encouraging. "You seem to know a lot more about investing than I do," he told Max. "I have never read Graham's book or Bogle's. I'm basically a salesman. My company's stock and bond analysts make buy and sell recommendations. I persuade my customers to go with the recommendations."

The next broker Max talked with sent his BS detector into screaming overdrive. The man claimed he could make Max a millionaire a hundred times over before he reached his senior years. Max thanked the broker for his time and left the guy's card on his desk as he departed the office.

Max's next stop was the world of mutual funds, a method of investing that was first offered to the public in 1924. Mutual funds buy and sell the stocks or bonds of a range of companies. Investors can, in turn, buy shares of the funds.

The managers of a mutual fund collect dividends from the companies whose stocks it has purchased. They collect interest on the bonds. They look to buy stocks or bonds at advantageous prices with an eye toward selling them at a profit – or, in investor-speak, a "capital gain." They try to sell investments that are going downhill before the losses become severe. (Some mutual funds churn their holdings at a frenetic rate, turning over their entire portfolio several times a year. Others turn over only small portions of their portfolio annually.)

After collecting fees for their services, the funds share the dividends, interest, and gains among their investors. For stock and bond investors the fees are a big problem. For any one year they may appear trivial. But over the long haul, the fees soak up a huge portion of an investor's capital. In our chapter "Friction, Debt, Max, and Taxes," we saw how even a seemingly innocuous fee of 1 percent can greatly reduce investment gains.

Enter John Bogle, the founder of Vanguard financial services and the creator of what is called "the index fund." Bogle began his career working in the mutual fund industry. He was angered by what he saw: Mutual funds skimmed off fees – sales fees, management fees, and marketing and distribution fees adding up to far more than 1 percent – at every turn. The result was that folks who entrusted their savings to traditional mutual funds (TMFs) enjoyed far less benefit than they should have. Bogle calculated that investors realized only two thirds of what they would have gained had there been no fund managers between them and the stock and bond markets. The mutual fund managers helped themselves to the other third.

Bogle summarized his take on the mutual fund industry in a single word: "predatory." He set out to provide everyday investors with a way to enjoy gains near to those produced by the stock market itself. He created the first index fund.

An index fund differs from traditional mutual funds in this key respect: TMFs are actively managed. Their managers, like brokers, do research in an attempt to identify stocks and bonds they believe will enjoy outsized gains and to avoid losers. The managers of index funds have a much simpler job. They simply maintain a portfolio that matches in its composition all the stocks or bonds in an "index" – a hypothetical portfolio consisting of a defined range of stocks or bonds.

The best-known index includes the 500 largest U.S. companies. A 500 index fund owns shares in all of the companies in the 500 index. Among other index funds are those that own shares of a range of smaller, midsize, or international companies. Still others own a range of bonds.

Because they are passively managed rather than actively managed like TMFs, index funds do not need to charge the burdensome fees exacted by the TMFs. That is not to say index funds are entirely frictionless. They do require some management. That management does cost money.

The difference between the management fee for index funds and TMFs is huge. These days TMF fees range from 0.5 percent to 2.5 percent. That ads up to $5,000 to $25,000 per decade for management of a $100,000 investment. By contrast, the fee for the Vanguard 500 index fund (as of early 2021) is 0.04 percent – four hundredths of one percent annually. That amounts to a $40 a year and just $400 per decade for a $100,000 investment in the fund.

Let me repeat that: You give $100K to a fund manager (or, for that matter, a broker). They will charge you $5K, $10K, or even $25K to manage it for a decade. An index fund will run you a few hundred dollars. As you know from our discussions of compounding in "Investment Literacy II," such a difference in fees can make a gigantic difference in investor gains over the course of years.

To make matters worse, there's practically no chance, as we will discuss in a few paragraphs, that you will get better results from the high-priced manager or broker than from the dirt-cheap index fund.

The same math holds true for "exchange traded funds (ETFs)," a more recent innovation in the world of investment products. ETFs are in major respects nearly identical to parallel index funds. For example, the Vanguard 500 ETF holds the same shares as the Vanguard 500 Index. A primary difference is this: You can buy and sell an ETF at any time the marketplace for stocks and bonds is open for business and at the price in effect at the time you choose to sell. You can buy or sell an index fund only at the valuations that are established at the time the markets close for the day.

Along with fees, stock and bond investing poses other burdens and drawbacks. A relationship with stocks and bonds is strictly mathematical. You have no relationship at all with the people who work in the companies that provide you with income. There is no personal connection such as you can enjoy with tenants.

Stock and bond investing can impose a moral challenge. You may find yourself investing in companies whose products or practices you find reprehensible. Are you concerned about the hazards to human health posed by sugar? If you invest in a 500 index or ETF fund, you will be investing in companies that produce the sugary drinks that, according to one study, cause the death of some 184,000 people a year. Do you object to the use of alcohol or tobacco and to investment in companies that produce cigarettes or alcoholic beverages? Or to companies that shift production overseas? If you invest in conventional index funds or ETFs, you will be investing in such companies.

To evade moral hazard, you can choose to invest in a fund that refrains from putting capital into the kinds of businesses you don't like. Investors do increasingly have available such funds, including index funds. They exclude various categories of goods or services from their holdings. Whether you lean left or right politically, you likely will be able to find a fund that excludes companies providing goods or services you find objectionable.

When Max turned away from doing stock selection for himself and moved toward investing in funds, he began with TMFs. He was startled to learn how badly the fund managers served their clients. For all their churning of their holdings, TMFs virtually never did perform better than comparable indexes. Not over any significant period of time. A study Max came across had followed TMFs that had been given a five-star rating by a prominent provider of investing data. After they received their five stars, the funds proceeded to underperform their indexes by 7 percent to 11 percent over the following decade.

Another study reviewed the performance of several thousand funds relative to the 500 index. It reported that only one out of fifty, a miserable 2 percent, had outperformed – i.e., registered greater gains than – the index over the preceding decade. The other 98 percent had underperformed. Reading that, Max saw that trying to choose a TMF that would outperform was like looking over a herd of dairy cows wandering around in their pasture and trying to guess which would produce the most milk over the next ten years.

Max's conclusion (and mine, too, btw): Putting money into TMFs is, to put it politely, a dubious proposition. You'll spend a lot of time pouring over newsletters and financial magazines trying to locate outperforming funds. You are highly unlikely to receive compensation for your efforts. Ditto for working with a broker. How can you determine which broker even matches, much less does better than, the indexes and will do so going forward? You can't.

The bottom line: Putting capital in index funds with super low management fees is likely to be the most efficient and effective way for you to invest in stocks and bonds. You can, in effect, purchase shares in a large part of the U.S. and even the entire world economy. That economy has its downs along with its ups. But to date people who have invested in it and stayed the course have become vastly better off financially than those who have not.

Then there's that additional benefit, the one Max discovered: Unlike rentals whether residential or commercial, laundromats or individual stocks, index funds require virtually no management by their owner. You may want to occasionally rebalance them so that you maintain a proportion of stock to bond funds that you are comfortable with. That requires only a trivial amount of time. Acquire a nice chunk of the world economy via index funds or ETFs and you have become about as financially free as it is possible to be.

If you do decide to invest in index funds, you'll face one more question: Which funds should you choose? Different financial advisors suggest differing strategies. They range from simple to complex. A simple strategy, one suggested by Vanguard, is settling on just four index funds: The U.S. total stock market index, the U.S. intermediate term (as opposed to long or short term) bond index, an international stock index, and an international bond index.

The most complex selection I have seen includes ten index funds. On the stock side, they range from index funds holding stocks for large companies to those holding stocks for small companies. On the bond side, a similar variety is included. The recommendation also calls for keeping equal amounts of money in each of the ten funds. And it urges regular rebalancing – moving money from one fund to another as they grow or shrink at different rates – so that you maintain an equal amount of money in each of your ten funds.

Max adopted neither strategy. He reminded himself that his goal was to strengthen and protect his financial freedom. For that he needed cash flow and a portfolio that was simple to manage, in need of only occasional adjustment. He first invested in "value" index funds that produced relatively large dividends. Only after some years, when his cash flows greatly exceeded his needs, did he begin diversifying into a broader range of index funds.

Though other companies also offer index funds, Max elected to go with Vanguard exclusively. Ever attentive to using time efficiently, he wanted to have all his investments at a single financial firm rather than having to look over statements and reports from several. He was taken with Vanguard's library of free brochures. Unlike the publications of other investment firms, the Vanguard stuff felt to Max like education, not like a sales pitch.

Max was impressed by Bogle's design for the company he had founded. Bogle had set up the company so that shareholders are, in effect, the owners of the company. Its managers are not the owners, other than to the extent that they invest in Vanguard funds, nor is any outside investor. Therefore, the managers are legally responsible to their shareholders, not to outsiders. "Nice," thought Max. Kind of like the thinking behind running an employee centered company. Enlightened self-interest, not greed. It has worked; Vanguard has 30 million owners, i.e., the people who hold shares in its funds.

At the outset, Max made use of dollar cost averaging – the technique described in our chapter on deploying capital. He invested monthly at a steady rate, not paying attention to whether the market valuations were up or down. In time, however, Max began holding off from investing in stock funds when prices became too "frothy" to use investor lingo, i.e., when they were reaching irrational or historically unprecedented levels. He saw that stocks purchased during those times took decades to recover value after a market crash.

To distinguish crazy high markets from reasonable markets, Max made use primarily of a chart produced by Robert Shiller. The chart is available at a website listed in "Tools." It displays changes over the last century in the ratio of the price of the 500 index to the earnings of the companies in the index.

The use of price-to-earnings ratios (PE) is commonplace in stock investing. However, the usual PE considers only a past year's earnings. If a stock fund is selling for $100 a share and the average earnings per share of the companies in the fund is five dollars over the past year, then the PE for the fund is 20 ($100 \div 5 = 20$).

Earnings of companies can fluctuate massively from year to year. For that reason, one-year PEs are of limited value. To provide something more useful, Shiller's chart makes use of what is technically known as "cyclically adjusted price earnings" or CAPE. Price is compared not to just one year's worth of earnings but to the average earnings over the past ten years. If the price of a share of a 500 index fund is $175 and earnings over the past ten years have averaged $5 a share, then CAPE is 35 (175 ÷ 5 = 35).

In fact, 35 is where CAPE stood when I first wrote these lines; and it was approaching 40 when I last edited them. A CAPE of 40 is the second highest of all time and more than twice the historical average. That's not Max's kind of market. He has heard people justifying the high prices just as he had heard elaborate rationalizations for the stratospheric stock market valuations of the later 1990s. He ignored them. "Margin of safety," he reminded himself. He was content to stockpile cash until the next steep market drop. Inevitably it would come, he believed. When it did, he'd resume dollar cost averaging.

As you know from an earlier chapter, Max's strategies worked out for him. He enjoyed an unusual level of financial freedom beginning early in his career.

Max felt fortunate. He did not congratulate himself. When asked for the secret to his success, he said "Luck." After he had said "luck" repeatedly during an interview for a builders' magazine, the journalist challenged him. "Surely it was more than luck? Ability? Hard work? Courage?"

"Luck is the big factor," Max insisted. He reeled off times he had been lucky: Getting pulled into the fascinating world of construction when he was seeking a career during his youth. Settling in an area where reliable builders were in high demand and where you could make good money. Buying a home during a depressed market so that he got it at a low price and was able to soon pay off his mortgage. As a result of that, being able to rapidly accumulate capital to put into cash flowing investments.

Maybe the luckiest events of all: Coming across mentors among his fellow builders and in books and journals who taught him sound business practices. Coming across other mentors who helped him learn how to evaluate and buy investment real estate. And then still others who, when he needed to diversify beyond rentals, guided him away from seeing stock and bond investing as mere gambling and toward investing into index funds.

"Yeah," Max told the interviewer, "Maybe part of my luck came my way because of who I am. I'm persistent. But there's some luck there, too. When I was younger, I didn't know how to persist. I got angry and frustrated. I lost my temper and quit. Fortunately, I ran into some teachers like John Bogle who drove home this lesson: Never quit.

"And yeah, I'm organized. I'm frugal; I like not wasting stuff, getting good stuff that lasts. But I was taught that, too. By my parents. They had their act together. They lived well. But they used their resources thoughtfully. They minimized waste.

"So maybe it's all luck," he told the interviewer. "It's who you get for family. Who you happen to meet. Who you happen to listen to. It's where you are born and where you land. It's which information or opportunity comes along and nudges you this way or that. It's marrying a person, as I happened to, who stands by you, who encourages you, who puts up with your quirks, who guides you toward good decisions. Yep, the way I see it, success is just about all luck, at least in my case."

At times when Max was reflecting on the good luck he had enjoyed in his career, he would think about Oliver. Happening into Oliver, that was an early moment of good fortune. Oliver had hired him onto the best construction job he'd had during his apprenticeship. Building two houses with Oliver had consolidated his construction skills. Not only had he developed carpentry skills, he had observed how the different trades came and went during a project. By the time he moved on to his next job, he understood how all the systems in a house were fitted together. He understood the sequencing of the work. Though he did not realize it at the time, he had taken a big step toward becoming a builder in his own right.

Max often wondered how life had gone for Oliver since he'd last seen him – the day Oliver visited Max's home and angrily spoken about the bank's foreclosure of his projects. In later years, Max sometimes vacationed with his family in the hill town where Oliver had built his house above the river. He asked around about Oliver. He queried real estate brokers and construction guys, "Do you remember a guy named Oliver Williams? Really good builder, used to work up here?" No one recognized the name.

Sometimes Max would speculate about Oliver's path. He doubted that Oliver had stayed down for long. He had been more pissed off than defeated that day when he had stepped out of his International Harvester pickup at Max's project. Max imagined that the anger would have fueled a comeback of some kind. He wondered what it might have been.

Maybe, Max speculated, Oliver had adopted his father-in-law's strategy: Build a house. Don't build another till it's sold. Invest your profits in real estate. Repeat. Or maybe he had resumed development, but this time recruiting private investors who would ride through the ups and downs rather than abandoning or crushing the builder, as banks could and did when markets turned south.

Perhaps, Max thought, Oliver had found an entirely different path for himself. Maybe he was now a banker making loans to builders instead of taking out loans. Or perhaps he had started a company providing software for builders.

Or maybe, Max would sometimes worry, Oliver had a job site accident. Maybe he was gone, like other of Max's friends who had been taken long before they were old. He wished he could find out how life had gone for the guy who had helped him take such a big step forward in his own career. Eventually he did, though as it turned out, none of Max's guesses about the direction Oliver's life had taken were on target.

Epilogue: Beyond Financial Freedom

Recently, I told a friend a story about a builder who had an uncommon bit of luck. He removed the drywall in an old cottage and discovered stacks of gold bricks between the studs. The friend said, "That'll sure put him on Easy Street."

"Maybe," I thought. Though sometimes, with luck, you do hit long smooth stretches of road, I am not sure there is an Easy Street through life. It is not the street I found after reaching financial freedom. I got to it at a modest level during my thirties. By then I had enough money from investments to cover my minimal financial obligations and needs.

From there, I gradually made my way to the point that I felt my freedom would endure any but the direst of circumstances – say, climate change-induced flood, fire, and storm, combined with the outbreak of a nuclear war. I do not discount such possibilities. They appear to me to be real. But I was willing to ignore them, at least with respect to my personal situation. You can't build financial freedom so secure it will hold up through the apocalypse, should it come.

With it secured against pretty much anything but doomsday, I gradually rolled up my company and supported my employees in finding new jobs or starting their own companies. I declared myself "retired."

That moment began the worst four months of my life, a period of feeling useless, bored, disconnected from community, anxious, depressed, discarded, and drained of energy. It was genuinely awful.

I arrived at a conclusion about myself. I suspect it may be valid for many readers of this book on the way to the point they won't have to work for monetary reasons. When you get there, you have to fill your freedom with meaning. You may imagine that once you are free, life will transform into uninterrupted effortless contentment. That you will get up each morning, stretch and yawn, brew a cup of coffee, enjoy a slow breakfast with the newspaper, mosey over to the club for eighteen holes or a doubles match, get a massage, and kick back for an evening of NBA on the tube. Rest and repeat the next day. Now and then head off to Brazil, Belize, or Belgium to take a look around.

If you can pull that off, please let me know how you manage it. My guess is that you won't be able to. I asserted right at the outset of this book, the kind of person who has the drive to build financial independence needs something to push against. I continue to think that is likely. You have entrepreneurial energy and executive capability. You kept yourself on a steep learning curve for a long while and have a hungry mind.

Those capabilities and that curiosity need to be exercised as surely as your body does. You need to discharge your creative energies. Plus, the world needs you. There are countless people who could use a hand. There are a lot of problems out there that need attention.

I have used my own freedom for a series of building, writing, consulting, and investing projects that matter to me and that I hope have benefited others. Some have been lucrative. Many I have done pro bono. I am grateful for the freedom that allows me to do the work without being constrained by financial outcomes. I am equally grateful to have meaningful work to do.

Max had an experience similar to mine after reaching financial freedom. After a period of puzzlement and depression, he realized he needed to engage meaningfully with life. Looking back on his career, he remembered how hard he'd had to scratch around to acquire basic business knowledge. He was grateful for the mentors he had come upon, and, for that reason, Max decided to mentor aspiring young entrepreneurs in his post-freedom years.

Max spoke of the experience as a final stroke of luck in a blessed life. "You know how it is. It's just amazing, isn't it," he said to a friend who did similar work. "A student comes up and tells you they were struggling with their business, that you got them over the hump and that they are now doing well. It makes you feel like 'Hey, I did something with my life that mattered.'"

"I know the feeling, I know it," answered the friend. "It's the best."

The friend who said that to Max was Oliver. Half a century after they had worked building houses together for Oliver's father-in-law, and long after Max had all but forgotten about Oliver, he came upon him by chance. One evening he was browsing around on YouTube. He was hoping to find a presentation about the new model for delivering construction projects that emphasized collaboration between owner, designer, and builder.

Max did find a presentation. The speaker was a tall, trim man with steel-gray hair and an easygoing and confident way about him. He was emphasizing the need for the three parties to get out of their bunkers, ditch the old adversarial procedures for delivering construction projects, and learn how to collaborate for their mutual benefit. Max recognized the voice and then the face. "I'll be damned," he said out loud to himself. "Oliver."

Max adjusted the screen so he could see the title of the talk and the name of the speaker. Yes, Oliver Williams it was. Same guy, just with a more neatly trimmed beard.

Max searched out a listing for Oliver on the Internet. He was living above a river again and in another spacious home, this one along the eastern slope of the Rocky Mountains. Max phoned Oliver, got voice mail, described himself and asked whether he was leaving a message for the Oliver Williams he had built houses with so long ago. Oliver called back the next day. He and Max talked for hours, sharing memories, stories of their careers in construction, their ideas for improving the industry, and their personal lives.

After losing his houses to the bank, Oliver had searched for ways to make enough money to support his family. Half a year later, a friend invited him to partner up in a new company building out stores for a national sporting goods chain. When that work ended, Oliver decided to put to rest his career as a general contractor. He took a job as a supervisor for a commercial construction outfit.

Oliver ascended as rapidly along his new career path as he had as a builder. But this time he did not get derailed. He rose through the ranks until he was managing the design and construction of major facilities from fire department stations to college sport centers. He began teaching at university construction management programs and became head of a national organization devoted to raising standards and performance across the industry.

Max and Oliver agreed that they had been fortunate to find their way to construction. They had not been destined for it. Oliver had been encouraged by his family to go into the military. He had worked as an aide-de-camp for an admiral before deciding Navy life was not for him. Max had been pushed by his college professors to follow in their footsteps and enter a doctoral program in the biological sciences. He cringed at the thought of spending his life cooped up in labs. He left college to learn to build.

Max and Oliver had both found construction endlessly engaging. You were always on the move, not going to work in the same place day after day, decade after decade. You could make good money. You did work that really mattered to other people, building shelter for their family, community, and work lives.

You were endlessly challenged as you climbed the construction industry ladder. As an apprentice and then journeyman, you had to learn how to fit things together. As manager of your jobs and then your office, you had to learn how fit processes together. As an executive, running your own company and developing projects for clients, you had to learn how to choose and position people so that they meshed with one another. If you wanted to arrive at financial independence, you had to learn how to assemble assets that complemented each other. And finally, as a mentor, you tried to find ways to help people fit better with their purpose, possibilities, and principles.

"And after all that," Max observed with mock complaint, "you find out you can't just kick back. You have to keep going and fill up all that free time you have created for yourself. How has that gone for you?"

"Yeah," said Oliver, "Well, it's not been easy. It's hard. You have to learn to slow down. At the same time, you have to find a way to stay stimulated and engaged and helping other people. I'm getting the hang of it. Hey, I wouldn't trade this for anything. I love being able to get up in the morning and decide how I want to spend the day. I'm living my best life."

"I don't have anything to add to that," Max answered.

Tools

AT WEBSITES
Robert Shiller's charts for CAPE (cyclically adjusted price/earnings ratio) and other metrics for evaluating stock prices at http://www.multpl.com/shiller-pe
The CAPE chart displays fluctuations in the market valuation of the 500 index divided by earnings over the previous ten years. The changes are calculated using real, i.e., inflation-adjusted dollars. The chart can help an investor determine whether market prices for the 500 index are at historically moderate, low, or high levels.

Ninety year 500 index chart at https://www.macrotrends.net/2324/sp-500-historical-chart-data
The chart displays the rise and fall of the market value of the 500 index over ninety years in real, i.e., inflation adjusted, dollars. It provides a sobering view of just how long it takes stock markets to recover after crashing from an extreme high. Thereby, it can help investors resist getting caught up in crazed, speculative markets.

Financial calculators at https://www.investor.gov
Under the Financial Tools and Calculators tab you will find several calculators that are useful for construction pros (or anyone else) seeking financial freedom. I made use of the Compound Interest

Calculator for the calculations in the text that illustrate the power of compounding.

Article on discounting to present day value at https://www.investopedia.com/terms/p/presentvalue.asp

The idea behind discounting to present day value (PV) is that to meaningfully evaluate the current, i.e., present day, worth of an investment one must determine what it is going to return over the coming years. Performing PDV calculations is not for the mathematically timid. If you want to give it a try, the Investopedia article will thoroughly acquaint you with the concept and provide you with the necessary formula.

Ibbotson charts of long-term returns at https://static.twentyoverten.com/59384d067cdd6a62d6fcc61f/pDJb2Hh_ux0/DSWM-Long-Term-Market-Returns.pdf

George Ibbotson was a professor of finance at Yale. His charts provide a fascinating visual account of the performance of different asset classes over time. I have provided a link to one collection of the Ibbotson charts here. Google "Morningstar Ibbotson Charts" and you can find many more.

FROM DAVID GERSTEL'S BOOK

On the following pages I have provided two forms and two lists from my book *Nail Your Numbers: A Path to Skilled Construction Estimating and Bidding*:

- **Labor productivity record. Reliable** records of productivity for items of work at past jobs are essential for accurate estimating of labor costs on upcoming jobs. The sample included here is number eleven of twenty labor productivity records included in *Nail Your Numbers*.

- **Included/Not included form for** use with trade partners. I have found this form helpful for preventing items of work from falling between the estimates provided by trade partners.
- **List of sources of** profit costs. There are a lot of them!
- **Site inspection checklist. This** is one of many checklists needed by a well-organized construction pro.

> DAVID GERSTEL / BUILDER
>
> Labor Productivity Record #11

ITEM OR ASSEMBLY: Wall Frame for New Construction
Included: Layout, sill, plates, headers, studs, plumb, line, brace.
NIC: Sheathing.

QUANTITY & DEGREE OF DIFFICULTY of ITEM: 510 l.f. standard 8'-high walls. Simple new construction job; a basic box with simple floor plan. Green lumber; good stock required little culling.

PROJECT: Single-story home. Adcock Avenue.
TIME OF CONSTRUCTION: Fall
CLIENT: Emerson. A++ Client. Fair & appreciative. Nice to work with.
DESIGNER: Peggy Simpson. Great to work with. Clear plans. Responsive to RFIs. Respectful.

ACCESS: Good parking. Close in staging area. Uncluttered site.
WEATHER: Sunny mostly. Some rain at night; site dried quickly.
OTHER FACTORS: Hand nailing.

CREW CAPABILITY:
    Lead: Guido R – "The Natural."
    Journeymen: Whitey C. – solid.
    Apprentice: Julia – Topnotch.
    Laborer: None

HOURS PER CREW PERSON:
    Lead: 110 hrs.
    Journeymen: 121 hrs.
    Apprentice: 106 hrs.
        TOTAL HOURS: 337

HOURS PER UNIT: ⅔ hrs./ft.

A Generic Included/NIC Checklist

Subcontractor: _____ Sub's Signature: _____

Project: _____

Our bid is based on the following plans and specifications for the above-named project:

Architectural Plans, pages _____ Date: _____

Engineering Plans, pages _____ Date: _____

Specifications, pages _____ Date: _____

Addenda, pages _____ Date: _____

Our bid includes **all** work and costs regularly, *though not necessarily always*, covered by our trade **excepting items checked below** to indicate they are not included (NIC).

Building permit _____	Provide roof jacks _____	Touchup paint _____
Shop drawings _____	Provide straps _____	
Liability insurance _____	Provide roof caps _____	Other items of work and costs NIC in our bid:
Workers Comp Insurance _____	Install jacks, caps, & straps _____	
Trench & backfill _____	Material handling _____	
Off-haul excess soil _____	Remove waste _____	
Demolition _____	Recycle _____	
Concrete cut/core _____	Protect (E) work _____	
Cut and patch _____	Blocking _____	
Scaffolding/Staging _____	Firestops _____	
Ramps _____	Insulation _____	
Ladders _____	Sealants & caulk _____	
Damage repair _____		
Utility hookups _____	Touchup drywall _____	
Flashing _____	Daily cleaning _____	
	Final cleanup _____	

Sources of Profit Costs

Before Construction Begins
- Item(s) overlooked during estimating
- Underestimating cost of items
- Bids leading to jobs beyond your capability
- Bids resulting in a volume of work beyond your capacity
- Delays caused by building departments
- Delays caused by designers
- Client delay or cancelation of a project
- Underpricing jobs to stay busy

During Construction
- Abrupt inflation of material costs during a job
- Contradictory or incomplete plans or specs
- Change order conflict
- Project halted due to inadequacies in design
- Projects halted due to client indecision
- Freebies to placate upset clients
- Layout errors
- Weather delays and disruptions
- Labor shortages or strikes
- Bankruptcy of subs
- Suppliers failing to deliver material on time
- Defective material

After Construction
- Warranty and goodwill work
- Major failures
- Bad debt and bandit clients

Anytime
- A client damages your reputation via social media
- Key personnel leave your company
- You or other key personnel become ill
- Theft
- Vandalism
- Accidental equipment or vehicle destruction
- Computer and software breakdown
- Embezzlement
- Tax and insurance audit penalties
- Recession
- Litigation
- Bankruptcy

Site Inspection Checklist

Prepare
- Schedule inspection with owner
- Schedule with subs
- Schedule consultants

Bring
- Overalls
- Rain gear
- Boots
- Gloves
- Dust mask
- Hardhat
- Hand tools (shovel, pick bar)
- Flashlight
- Project binder/laptop
- Note paper and pencils
- Camera
- Ladder
- Documents for subs
- Lunch

Off Site Factors to check
- Roadways
- Emergency medical
- Travel for crew
- Accommodations for crew
- Availability and capacity of suppliers
- Availability of subs
- Availability of temp labor
- Waste and recycling
- Distance to rental yards
- Licenses, taxes and local codes

Site Factors to check
- Access
- Parking
- Weather (during time of job!!!)
- Water
- Power
- Sanitary facilities
- Power lines
- Soil
- Grade
- Barricades
- Fences
- Tool and equipment security
- Site security
- Traffic control
- Erosion control
- Dust control
- Drain system protection
- Trees and plant protection
- Driveway protection
- Other exterior protection
- Grubbing
- Streams
- Area for material drops
- Excavated earth stockpile area
- Waste and recycle storage area
- Operating space for off-hauling
- Opportunities to use heavy equipment (cranes, etc)
- Distractions

Existing Building Factors to check
- Access
- Mobilization
- Interior protection
- Special protection (computers, art)
- Hidden demolition and deconstruction
- Material layers
- Vulnerable existing pipes
- Vulnerable existing windows
- Other vulnerable items
- Plumb, level, and square
- Difficult to reach framing and framing cavities
- Space for HVAC, plumbing, and electrical runs
- Tie-ins, structural
- Tie-ins, finish
- Condition of finishes
- Matching issues
- Reuse possibilities
- Health and safety hazards
- Accuracy of as-built dimensions
- Space for temporary facilities for owner

Additional Design/Build and Cost Planning Issues
- As-built dimensions
- Existing structural
- Existing HVAC
- Existing plumbing
- Existing electrical
- Existing drainage
- Existing decay
- Existing code violations
- Window and door locations
- Existing exterior finish
- Existing interior finishes incl. hardware
- Other as-built conditions

Essential Resources

GREAT BOOKS

The Intelligent Investor by Ben Graham. A justly revered classic full of essential guidance regarding the use of investment capital.

Bogle on Mutual Funds: New Perspectives for the Intelligent Investor by John Bogle. Here Bogle lays out the reasons for investing in index funds rather than traditional mutual funds.

VALUABLE BOOKS

Building the Affordable House by Fernando Pagés Ruiz. A tour de force in the exercise of frugality in home design and construction.

Construction Contractors' Survival Guide by Thomas Schleifer. I recommended it to my mentor, the extraordinary builder Deva Rajan. He told me that he reads it cover to cover at the start of every year. Judith Miller, a financial strategist who works with builders all over the country, describes it as her favorite book about the construction business. Enough said.

Investing in Real Estate by Gary Eldred. I consider Eldred's book the best resource on real estate investing I have found. It is comprehensive, readable, and engaging. It has much to offer seasoned investors and is invaluable for folks new to real estate investing.

The Millionaire Next Door by Thomas Stanley and William Danko. A thorough account of the values and practices of people who become and stay wealthy.

Small Giants by Bo Burlingham. A compelling account of outstanding smaller companies and their practices.

Own Your Own Corporation by Garrett Sutton. A clear guide to incorporation, its benefits, requirements, and burdens.

Total Money Makeover by David Ramsey. Though more about personal finance than business, Ramsey's book is inspirational about frugality, cash management, and the benefits of investing in the stock market. It provides clear procedures for the snowball method of debt reduction. It has been fairly criticized for overstating the benefits investors are likely to enjoy as a result of compounding.

OTHER BOOKS BY DAVID GERSTEL

Running a Successful Construction Company
Nail Your Numbers: A Path to Skilled Construction Estimating and Bidding.
Crafting the Considerate House

Reviews of these books at Amazon can help you decide if any would be useful for you.

ARTICLES

By Paul Eldrenkamp. Go to the *Journal of Light Construction* at *JLConline.com*. Type "Paul Eldrenkamp" in the search bar and you will be taken to Eldrenkamp's articles. They are concise and clear, and the advice they offer on running a construction company is as sound as any you will ever find.

By David Gerstel. My *Journal of Light Construction* articles are posted at DavidGerstel.com and can be found at *JLConline.com*. Among them is an article about the Splinter Group and several other associations where construction pros learn from one another.

Journal of Light Construction at https://www.jlconline.com. *JLC* makes its past articles available without charge online. The many business articles it has published over the decades since it was founded are generally sound and useful. Some, like Paul Eldrenkamp's (see above), are outstanding.

PODCASTS

Bogleheads at https://bogleheads.podbean.com.
The host of Bogleheads and his guests are knowledgeable and thoughtful professional investors. By listening to them you can acquaint yourself with variations on the investing strategies taught by Benjamin Graham and John Bogle.

Building Optimal Radio at buildingoptimal.com.
Jared Gossett, the host, is a custom home builder and remodeler in Austin, Texas. His podcasts go into unusual depth on major construction business issues. Several people, including Wally Staples and Fernando Pagés Ruiz, whom you met in this book, have appeared as guests on *Building Optimal Radio*, as have I.

The Tim Faller Show at thetimfallershow.com.
Tim Faller, the host, is a former remodeler who has worked for decades as an educator in the construction industry. His show focuses on production issues, with Tim mixing in sage and good-humored advice on business matters.

Power Tips Unscripted at powertipspodcast.com.
Hosted by Victoria Downing, the head of Remodelers Advantage, *Power Tips* offers lively, concise interviews about a broad range of business issues. Podcast #39, with financial strategist Judith Miller as guest, is an exceptionally good discussion of the pros and cons of growth.

WEBSITE ABOUT ESOPS

A good introduction to ESOPs is available at https://www.menke.com/esop-information/esop-information-library/

Glossary

Accounting – Keeping financial records.

Accrual accounting – Entering income and expenses into financial records when income is earned and expense is incurred (see the alternative, cash accounting, below).

Actively managed mutual fund – A mutual fund whose managers buy and sell stocks and bonds in an effort to maximize gains.

All-weather portfolio – A portfolio of investments designed to lose relatively little value during down markets and register gains during rising markets.

Alpha – Investment gains substantially in excess of those achieved by a broad market.

Bid – An attempt to win a contract for construction.

Bonds – As used in this book, "bonds" refers to a form of investment (as opposed to performance and license bonds required for construction). A bond is essentially a loan. Investors who buy a bond are making a loan to the company or government agency that issued the bond and in return receive interest and a promise to return the loan amount by a certain date.

Cap rate – the rate of return on a real estate investment that is determined by dividing the net income from the investment by its purchase price.

Capital reserves account – An account that can be drawn upon to cover unexpected expenses and losses.

Capital gain – A profit made on the sale of an investment such as stocks or real estate.

Capital gains tax – A tax on a capital gain.

Cash-on-cash return – The rate of return on the cash an investor has put into an investment.

Cash accounting – Entering income and expenses into financial records when income is received and expenses paid (see the alternative, accrual accounting, above).

Change order – An amendment to a construction contract that changes the scope of work, charges, and schedule called for in the contract.

Construction pro – As used in this book, "construction pro" refers primarily to a person who sets up their own company to provide construction services.

Cyclically adjusted price earnings (CAPE) – The price of an index divided by the average inflation adjusted earnings of the companies in the index over the previous ten years.

Direct costs – The costs of construction for labor, material, services, and trade partners (subcontractors) that are incurred at a work site.

Dividend – A payment, generally a portion of its profit, made by a company to its shareholders.

Dollar cost averaging (DCA) – Making investments in an asset periodically rather than in one lump sum.

Dow – Short for Dow Jones Industrial Average. The Dow is an index that includes the thirty largest U.S. companies listed on the stock exchanges. The Dow average is figured each day by adding up the stock prices of all of the thirty companies and dividing by a divisor adjusted for a variety of factors.

Draw – A term many construction pros use to refer to the pay or salary they take from their company.

Equity – Stocks or shares that provide ownership interest in a company. In real estate, the value of a property in excess of debt on the property.

Estimate – As used in this book, a reliable forecast of the costs of a construction project.

Exchange – A marketplace such as the New York Stock Exchange (NYSE) where stocks are listed for sale and are bought and sold.

Exchange traded fund (ETF) – A fund that owns stocks, bonds, or other types of investments. ETFs differ from index funds in that they can, like stocks, be bought or sold on an exchange at any time the exchange is open. Index funds can typically be bought or sold only after the exchange has closed for the day.

Frictional costs – The costs of a transaction such as brokerage or government fees beyond the cost of the goods being bought and sold.

Index fund – A mutual fund whose portfolio of investments matches the portfolio of a specific index, i.e., range, of stocks, such as those of the 500 largest U.S. companies.

Income statement – An accounting report that shows a company's income and expenses for a particular period of time, such as a month, quarter or a year; also known as a profit and loss statement.

Inflation – An increase in costs of goods and the resulting fall in purchasing power of money. In other words, when inflation occurs, you get less for a buck.

Internal rate of return (IRR) – A measurement of future financial performance that takes into account not only net income but other benefits such as tax shelter and possible appreciation.

Job costs – The actual costs of a construction project broken down by divisions of work such as concrete, framing, and windows.

Labor productivity – The amount of work accomplished in a unit of time, typically an hour, by a labor force of a certain size.

Labor productivity record – A record that shows the amount of work accomplished per hour by a labor force of a certain size working under specific conditions.

Margin of safety – Technically, margin of safety refers to making an investment at a market price that is below "intrinsic value" (as determined by calculating present value or by other formulations). Less technically, margin of safety refers to making an investment at a price such that the investor has a reasonable chance of a satisfactory return over time.

Market performance – Return on investment that is in line with the return that would have been achieved by investing in a broad market.

Metrics – Measurements.

Mutual fund – A fund whose managers pool money obtained from investors, invest the money in stocks, bonds, or other assets, and sell shares in the fund to investors.

Nominal dollars – Dollars whose value has not been adjusted for inflation and the resultant changes in purchasing power. To explain: Six dollars has the same nominal value in 1980 and 2020. But in 1980 the dollars have more real value, i.e., more purchasing power, than they will in 2020 because their purchasing power will have by then been weakened by inflation (See also "real dollars," below).

Out-of-pocket overhead – A term I use to describe the expenses, other than pay taken by the owner, of running a construction company.

Overhead – As used in this book, overhead refers to the costs, such as office expenses, of running a construction business as opposed to the direct costs for labor, material, etc. of building projects.

Owner's pay – The pay, also called "draw" or "salary," an owner takes for the work he does for his company.

Outperformance – Gains from investment that exceed the gains of a broad market.

Passively managed funds – Mutual funds, in particular index stock funds, whose managers maintain a portfolio that matches an index rather than trying to select investments that will outperform a market.

Payables – Bills such as payments due on a loan or invoices from suppliers or trade partners that have not yet been paid.

Portfolio – The collection of investments held by an investor.

Profit – The income a company retains after having paid all the costs and expenses associated with that income. Profit can be figured for an individual project or for a period of time such as a month, quarter, or year.

Profit costs – A term I invented to refer to the range of costs from fixing construction defects to lawsuits that can arise from a project long after it is completed. Profit costs have a family resemblance to what are termed "contingency costs." However, profit costs often come out of the blue and are entirely unanticipated, whereas contingency costs are often anticipated but of uncertain scope.

Profit and loss statement – An accounting report that shows a company's income and expenses for a particular period of time. Also known as an income statement.

Real dollars – Also known as constant dollars. Dollars whose value has been adjusted for inflation so that values at different times can be meaningfully compared (See "nominal dollars" above for further explanation).

Rebalance – Adjusting the holdings in a portfolio so that they are in line with a pre-set target such as 60 percent stocks and 40 percent bonds.

Receivables – Money owed to a business that it has not yet collected.

Security – A financial instrument such as a stock or bond that is issued by a business or government agency to raise capital.

Socially Responsible Fund – A mutual fund which excludes certain types of companies, such as those producing war materials, alcohol, fossil fuel, or tobacco, from its portfolio.

Salary – Pay for work, typically figured on a biweekly or monthly basis. Not to be confused with profit!

S&P 500 – Short for Standard and Poor 500, an index that includes the 500 largest U.S companies as weighted by market capitalization, i.e., the total value of the stocks of each of the companies.

Selling price – In the construction business, the amount of money a contractor initially agrees to charge an owner for construction of their project.

Spreadsheet – A sheet of paper or a computer screen that is divided into rows and columns to create a grid of cells, i.e., boxes, where information, particularly numbers, can be tabulated.

Stocks – Shares of ownership in a company. More technically known as an "equity security."

Time value of money – Refers to the fact that money received now is worth more than money received in the future, because the sooner money is received the sooner it can be invested to produce earnings.

Trade partners – A more respectful term that has in good part replaced the term "subcontractors."

Traditional mutual fund – A mutual fund with active management, namely one that seeks to outperform a market by buying and selling investments (see also "passively managed funds" and "outperformance").

Value engineering – Analyzing a project to figure out ways to cut cost while minimizing reduction in durability, aesthetic quality, or functionality.

Wages – Pay for work, typically figured on an hourly basis. Not to be confused with profit!

Appreciations and Acknowledgements

When a book is published, usually the name of just a single person appears on its cover. That person is known as "the author." I have long thought that most books really have several authors. That is certainly true for my books. I do type out the words that appear in the book. But other people have collaborated or even led the way in the thinking that underlies the words. Still others have shaped the sentences and suggested terminology.

For this book, the author team includes my wife Sandra, who read all the chapters and critiqued them as we read them aloud together. As a result of her interventions, many pages of obfuscation were cut and clarifications crafted.

Jackie Parente generously agreed to come out of retirement to provide substantive editing for *Building Freedom*, the third book we have authored together. As usual, she sharpened the focus of one chapter after another and stopped me from wandering off into excess repetition and insistence when the urge overcame me.

Pam Rosenthal and Michael Rosenthal of P&M Editorial Services provided the thorough copyediting and acute commentary that I have come to cherish over the course of working on two books and a dozen articles with them.

Deb Tremper of Six Penny Graphics created the cover and the interior layout and design as she has been doing for innumerable other books for decades.

Many other people have contributed to the thinking in the book via podcasts, conversation, interviews, and their own writings. They include Jared Gossett, Fernando Pagés Ruiz, and Steve Nicholls, three capable builders who are also industry educators; my superb co-workers and trade partners, especially Leslie Lacko, David Lassman, Fred Blodgett, and Jim Lunt; and Deva Rajan, the builder whom I looked to as a mentor for decades. Deva's encouragement has often helped me stay on my own path to freedom. His intertwined passions for the craft and business of building inspired me.

Max and Oliver, while choosing to remain anonymous, were generous in allowing me to share their stories. Readers of the book have wondered who they might actually be. About Oliver, I can only tell you that all guesses have been wildly off. About Max, the guesses vary. Some readers think he's a composite character. Others have assumed that he is a quasi-autobiographical character because his practices and values are much like my own. Still others have assumed Max is fictional and that Oliver is, too.

There may be something to all the guesses except for that last one. Neither Max nor Oliver is a fictional creation. I have altered a few details of place, time, and circumstance to preserve their anonymity. Every action and every thought I attribute to them occurred in the course of their careers. Both found great satisfaction in their work in the construction industry, contributed to its evolution, and, in their own and different ways, achieved financial freedom as well.

Index

access, 92, 93, 117, 119
accounting, 19, 20, 46-52, 89, 90, 99, 100, 103-105, 115, 123, 243, 244, 246, 248
accrual accounting, 243, 244
actively managed mutual fund, 216, 343
after-tax profit, 72
all-weather portfolio, 136, 137, 140, 146, 243
alpha (investor), 130-132, 243
American Institute of Architects, 86
Anchor Brewery, 117
appreciation of work, viii, 38, 41, 251
appreciation of real estate, 154, 197, 200-202, 207, 246
Armstrong World Industries (AWI), 131, 132, 143
arrogance
  of profitability, 10, 126
  of ignorance, 129, 165
articles, recommended, 240, 241
attorney. *See* lawyer
autonomy, 10, 38, 40, 82, 115
avalanche (debt), 164
AWI. *See* Armstrong World Industries

balance sheets, 51
bankruptcy, 51, 132, 149, 236
LaPatner, Barry, 25
Bean, L. L., 33

Berkshire Hathaway, 61, 131, 213
bids, 5, 18, 22, 39, 45, 70, 77, 86-100, 109, 179, 232, 236, 240, 243
Bitcoin, 141
Blodgett, Fred, 252
Bogle on Mutual Funds: New Perspectives for the Intelligent Investor, 239
Bogle, John, 16, 18, 129, 130, 155, 159, 212-216, 222, 239, 241
Bogleheads, 241
Bonds, U.S., 130, 131, 135, 136, 140, 154, 162, 169, 173, 212-218, 243, 245, 246, 248
books, recommended, 239, 240
brand, 4, 31, 80, 175
bubble, 149-151, 155, 159, 194
Buffett, Warren, 61, 129, 131, 132, 143, 146, 151, 213
build a brand, 80
Building Optimal Radio, 174, 241
Building the Affordable House, 81, 239
bureaucracy, 113
Burlingham, Bo, 180, 240
business management, 6, 22, 129
business plan, 59
business systems, 18, 20, 26, 56, 117, 164, 173

calculators, financial, 231

callbacks, 5, 50, 103, 105, 190
Canyon Construction, 175
cap rate. *See* capitalization rate
capacity/time method, 95-99
CAPE (see cyclically adjusted price earnings)
capital gain, 215, 244
capital gains tax, 244
capital reserves account, 126, 244
capitalization rate (cap rate), 200
Carnegie, Dale, 37
cash
   accounting, 243, 244
   flow, 19, 20, 27, 28, 100-104, 124, 126, 128, 142, 157, 186, 197, 200-203, 206-208, 219
   management, 105, 123, 240
   position, 101, 102, 104, 105
   reserves, 68, 72, 127, 128
   cash-on-cash return, 200, 201, 206, 207, 244
CBT (see cognitive behavioral therapy)
CDs (see certificates of deposit)
certificates of deposit (CDs), 120, 166
change order, 70, 85, 112, 236, 244
Schwarz, Charles, 30, 33
checklists, 12, 22, 23, 233
clients
   billing, 102
   contract, 20, 46, 78, 104, 108, 109, 203
   employee respect, 40-43, 76, 80, 115, 202
   free estimates, 85-87
   quality service, 31, 80, 86, 202
   problems, 5, 10, 48, 53, 54, 83, 109, 114, 179
   staying in contact, 29, 41, 77-80, 83, 113-115
   trust, 6, 93, 104
cognitive behavioral therapy (CBT), 46
cold calling, 75
communication, 20
compounding, 49, 144-146, 169, 170, 207, 216, 232, 240
consistent leadership, 24
constant dollars, 248
constructing profitability, 80, 83, 85

Construction Contractors' Survival Guide, 239
construction costs, 48, 94, 96
construction pro
   investments, 11, 132, 168, 170, 182, 194, 209, 211
   real estate, 132, 135, 168, 185-189, 194, 198, 200-202, 206-209, 211-213, 244
contingencies, 68, 70
contract
   bids, 243
   change order, 244
   construction, 20, 36, 39, 46, 59, 67, 75, 78, 80, 83, 85, 102, 104, 109, 112
   rental, 187, 190, 199, 203, 205
   preconstruction, 65, 115
contractor specials, 211
cost-effective use of resources, 30, 56
costs
   accounting, 89
   benefits, 56, 166
   billing, 102
   callbacks, 10
   construction, 54
   daily, 42
   direct costs, 47, 70, 97, 161, 244
   frictional costs, 161-163, 167, 245
   inflation, 246
   insurance, 110-113
   job costing reports, 109
   labor, 32, 92, 96, 232
   material, 32, 90, 189, 199, 236
   out-of-pocket, 7, 49, 67, 69, 186
   overhead, 247
   owners, 87, 119
   paring down, 30, 203
   profit, 33, 65, 70-72, 81, 101, 116, 117, 126, 176, 233, 248
   take-home pay, 68
   trade partners, 98
   See also real estate
COVID-19, 25, 59, 79, 205, 208
Crafting the Considerate House, 185, 240
creative energy, 1

Index

cryptocurrencies, 141
customers. *See* clients
customers for life, 82, 83
cutting corners, 31-33
cyclically adjusted price earnings (CAPE), 221, 231, 244

Dalio, Ray, 135-137, 140, 154
Danko, Bill, 27, 28, 240
DCA. *See* dollar cost averaging
debt
   avoidance, 30, 40, 174
   balance sheet, 104
   bankruptcy/bad debt, 149, 236
   interest, 125, 163-165
   investment, 131, 145, 194, 206, 208, 245
   reduction, 240
   risk, 27, 177, 178
decision-making, 1
design/build firm, 51, 58, 99, 173
designer, 10, 33, 37, 54, 71, 86, 92, 94, 115, 185, 227, 236
destructive thought pattern, 45, 46
determination, 16, 20, 39
digital marketing, 76, 77, 162
direct costs, 47, 70, 97, 161, 244, 247
discipline, 1, 156
distractions, 60, 61
diversify, 136-139, 159, 174, 194, 209, 219, 222
dividend, 132, 140, 155, 157, 167-169, 215, 219, 245
Dixon, Dennis, 86
dollar cost averaging (DCA), 155-157, 159, 167, 220, 221, 245
dollars, real, 146, 164, 247, 248
Dow. *See* Dow Jones Industrial Average
Dow Jones Industrial Average (Dow), 151, 245
Downing, Victoria, 127, 177, 241
draw, 65, 99, 124, 245, 247. *See also* pay
drive, 1, 17, 226
Duerfeldt, Treacy, 110, 111

earnings
   accounting, 89

earnings *(Continued)*
   capital, 21, 66
   corporate, 134, 150
   development, 164
   investment, 17, 40, 152
   loans, 102, 125
   present value (PV), 152-155, 201
   price-to-earnings ratio, 221, 231, 244. *See also* cyclically adjusted price earnings
   profit, 3
   stocks, 213, 220
   time value, 249
Edison, Thomas, 54
efficiency, 29, 32, 43, 75, 82, 84, 85, 165
Eldred, Gary, 125, 189, 190, 199, 204, 239
Eldrenkamp, Paul, 51, 93, 113, 126, 240, 241
embezzlement, 71, 103, 236
emotion, 152, 155, 157, 159, 199
employee centered, vii, 13, 35, 37-44, 79, 82, 220
employee stock ownership plan (ESOP), 176, 177, 183, 241
entrepreneur, 16, 17, 20, 23, 53, 59, 80, 134, 193, 194, 226, 227
environmental damage, 31
equity, 142, 186, 194, 208, 245, 249
ESOP. *See* employee stock ownership plan
estimating
   bidding, 90-94, 232, 240, 245
   charging, 7, 75, 85, 87, 109, 116
   checklist, 12, 22, 233
   errors, 67, 126, 129, 179, 180, 187, 205
   experience, 16
   job costing, 104
   overhead, 48
   procedures, 18-20, 77, 115, 175, 177
   profit, 69, 98, 236
   software, 36
   system, 18-20, 175, 177
   tracking costs, 100
ETFs. *See* exchange traded funds
ethics, ethical, 78, 99, 115

evaluating, 12, 18, 21, 24, 55, 56, 94, 110, 200, 231
Evening World, The, 54
eviction, 204, 205
exchange, 25, 217, 245
exchange traded fund (ETF), 217, 219, 245
executive, 5, 18, 226, 229

failure
 building, 17, 71, 81, 179, 199, 205, 236
 callbacks, 50
 hustlers, 130
 insurance, 109
 lack of capital, 21, 32
 litigation, 50
 monitor, 48
 opportunity, 7, 8
Faller, Tim, 11, 241
fear, 46, 93, 147, 152, 156
feedback loop, 38, 150, 158
financial freedom
 personal responsibility, iv
 drive, 1
 decision-making, 1
 discipline, 1
 investing, 2, 9, 41, 117, 128, 130, 133, 135, 219
 company ownership, 2
 passive investments, 2
 financial consultant/advisor, 10, 158, 162
 slow, but sure, 11, 160
 starting out, 16
 estimates, 18, 78, 90, 93, 94
 checklists, 22
 frugality, 28, 31, 32, 48, 52, 116, 182
 capital, 43, 61
 overhead, 49, 50,
 planning, 58, 59
 self-employment, 66
 profit, 72, 97
 debt, 102, 164
 insurance, 110
 taxes, 124, 125, 170
 overspending, 126

financial freedom *(Continued)*
 compounding, 144
 real estate, 152, 185, 188, 194, 198, 208, 209
 tools and calculators, 231
financial independence. *See* financial freedom
financial success, 3, 17, 29, 102
fixed percentage, 95, 96, 98
fixer uppers, 211
flow of money
 capital, 221, 100, 102, 126, 208
 cost control, 203
 inflow, 19, 20, 27, 124, 157
 outflow, 28, 101-103, 142
 portfolio, 219
 tracking, 104, 123, 126
foreclosures, 9, 108, 163, 194, 198, 199, 207, 208, 223
forms, 91, 232, 233
four-day workweek, 39, 41, 42
frictional. *See* costs
frothy, 220
frugality, 28, 30, 31, 65, 125, 167, 202, 239, 240

Gantt charts, 20, 21
general contracting, 67, 181
generosity, 3, 31, 33, 43
generous craftsman syndrome, 10
Gerstel, David, 183, 184, 232, 240
Gerstel, Sandra, 251
glossary, 243
goals, 59
gold, 43, 140, 141, 150, 225
Gossett, Jared, 86, 241, 252
GPM. *See* gross profit margin
Graham, Benjamin, 2, 24, 129-131, 133, 135, 140, 141, 143, 146, 147, 159, 212-214, 239, 241
Great Depression, 3, 7
gross profit margin (GPM), 94
grow or die, 50, 51
growth
 investments, 144-146, 168
 preparation, 113
 rate, 11, 58, 116-120, 180

growth *(Continued)*
  risks, 51, 101, 241
  taxes, 163

housing prices, 192-194
guarantees, 25, 157, 176, 207
handyman, 45, 202
hiring, 21, 22, 42, 176, 202, 209
Hoover Dam, 3, 8
hub-and-spoke operation, 177, 179-183
hubris, 11, 61
humility, 16

Ibbotson, George, 232
image, professional, 114
inbound marketing, 76
income statement, 246, 248
incorporation, 111, 112, 240
index fund, 215-222, 239, 245, 247, 248
inflation
  gold, 141
  impact, 136, 155, 166, 212, 236, 246-248
  real dollars, 146, 164, 192, 231
  See also cyclically adjusted price earnings
initial public offering (IPO), 149
inspection checklist, 22, 93, 233
insurance
  broker, 111, 112, 178, 202, 205
  liability, 109, 112
  workers' compensation, 109, 111
intangible costs, 93
Integrated Project Management, 86
Intelligent Investor, The, 2, 24, 129, 239
internal rate of return (IRR), 200, 201, 246
internet stocks, 134, 135, 141, 150
into-your-pocket expenses, 47
Investing in Real Estate, 239
investing, real estate, viii, 171, 185-239
investments
  capital, 25, 128, 151, 173, 188, 211, 239
  company ownership, 173
  compounding, 145-147
  diversity, 136, 139, 174, 182, 194, 209

investments *(Continued)*
  dollar-cost averaging, 155-157, 245
  financial pros, 131
  frugality, 28, 68
  gold, 140, 141
  incorporation, 111
  mutual funds, 155, 215, 249
  overhead, 49
  passive income, 2, 247
  portfolio, all weather, 243
  processes, 197
  profit, 50
  speculation, 144, 159, 160
  stocks, 131
  taxes, 168-170
  See also employee stock ownership plan
  See also investing, real estate
IPO (initial public offering), 149
IRR (see internal rate of return)

job costing, 104, 105
jobsite signs, 31, 114, 183
Journal of Light Construction, The, 17, 38, 51, 240, 241

Kolbert, Dan, 17
labor
  costs, 18, 232
  estimating, 92
  productivity, 18, 87, 93, 115, 232, 246
  productivity record, 246

lack of capital, 21, 22
Lacko, Leslie, 252
Lassman, David, 252
lawyers, 20, 111
leadership, 17, 18, 23-25, 42, 89
leads, 77, 78, 95, 103, 113, 115
lean practices, 15, 28-31, 33, 52, 103-105, 107, 115-117, 164, 167, 182, 206
learning curve, 5, 128, 226
leverage, 141-143, 206-208
limited liability corporations (LLCs), 112
listen, 3, 16, 76, 78, 130, 222, 241

litigation, 50, 205, 236
LLCs (see limited liability corporations)
Lost Arts Press, 30
luck, 9, 11, 17, 24, 25, 71, 108, 120, 178, 192-195, 221, 222, 225, 227
Lunt, Jim, 252

management systems, 6, 22
manager
  attention, 61
  company, 7
  competence, 17, 36
  efficiency, 84, 85, 115
  estimating, 92
  fees, 162
  hiring, 208
  money manager, 131, 158, 159
  overhead, 48
  pay, 69
  profit, 81
  property, 125, 209, 212
  stocks, 215-218, 243, 246, 247
  time, 99
margin of safety, 133-139, 145, 147, 151, 157, 159, 179, 201, 246
marketing
  callbacks, 5
  checklists, 22
  digital, 76, 77
  investing in, 31, 51
  kinds of, 55, 58, 75-79, 114
  leads, 77, 78, 103
  program, 17, 18, 20, 56, 90, 178
  rates, 67
  sharing knowledge, 133
market performance, 132, 246
market value, 136, 142, 162, 182, 193, 200, 202, 231
markets
  real estate, 193, 197, 199, 200-202, 211
  rental, 188, 189, 192, 194, 202
  stock, 194, 213-223, 231, 232, 243-249
material costs, 32, 90, 97, 236
Max, 1-12, 226-229, 252
Maytag, Fritz, 117
medical plan, 66

mentors, 6, 11, 17, 76, 78, 112, 129, 165, 169, 175, 213, 222, 227, 229, 239, 252
metrics, 135, 151, 231, 246
Miller, Judith, 126, 183, 239, 241
millionaires next door (MNDS), 27-29
Millionaire Next Door, The, 27, 28, 50, 170, 240
Mills, Sam, 35, 44
mind reading, 45
misconceptions, 46, 59
mistakes of commission, 8
mistakes of omission, 8
MNDS (see millionaires next door)
motion efficiency, 29
mutual funds, 130, 132, 155, 167, 168, 213, 215, 216, 239, 247

Nail Your Numbers: A Path to Skilled Construction Estimating and Bidding, 48, 93, 232, 240
net worth, 28, 51, 52, 104, 105
network, 4, 7, 17, 55, 165, 205
Nicholls, Steve, 173, 179, 180, 252
nominal dollars, 247, 248
numbers, 47-49, 57, 66-69, 72, 77, 87, 89-93, 100-105, 154, 155, 232, 240, 249. *See also* accounting

Oliver, 1-12, 226-229, 252
operating costs, 98, 199
opportunity, 7, 8, 10, 16, 17, 54, 59, 83, 95, 147, 194, 222
out-of-pocket expenses, 7, 47, 49, 50, 67-69, 120, 127, 186, 247
outflow of money, 100, 103
outperformance, 131, 247, 249
overhead
  costs, 47-49, 69, 70, 87, 94, 96-98, 103, 167, 179, 203, 247
  owner's pay, 65, 101
overhead obliviousness, 48, 50, 51
overimprovement strategy, 189
overreaching, 22, 120
overspecialization, 79
overspender, 126-128
overthinking, 53

Own Your Own Corporation, 240
owner
  balance sheet, 105
  behavior, 35-43, 54, 55
  buying/selling companies, 175-179, 182, 183
  debt, 163
  pay, 48-50, 65, 66, 75, 124, 127, 247
  profit, 73
  property, 142, 143
  rentals, 187, 198, 202, 203, 207, 209
  stocks, 213, 214, 219
  taxes, 168
  team, 86, 227

P&L. *See* profit and loss
Parente, Jackie, 251
passive investments, 2, 99, 131, 216, 247, 249
passively managed funds, 216, 247, 249
payments
  bidding, 127
  billing, 102
  contracts, 125
  dividends, 245
  flow of, 101
  interest, 36, 52, 164, 166, 174, 176, 182
  mortgages, 163, 194, 206
  nonpayment, 188
  payables, 247
  profit, 32
  software, 10
pay, personal, 67, 71, 124, 125, 128. *See also* owner's pay.
payables, 104, 105, 247
PE. *See* price-to-earnings ratios
Pearce, Duayne, 86
people policies, 21, 109
personal freedom, 31, 56, 60, 72, 124, 125, 128, 225, 228
planning, 57, 58
PM. *See* production manager
podcasts, list of, 241
points, 19, 78, 161
points of separation, 78
portfolio
  all-weather, 140, 243
  compounding, 169
  construction pro, 137
  diversification, 136, 145, 146, 167, 174, 182, 209
  financial advisor, 162
  gold, 141
  mutual funds, 130
  passive investments, 2, 147
  property, 142, 157
  stocks and bonds, 147, 155, 168, 214-216, 219, 245, 248
possibilities
  financial, 32
  compounding, 49
  debt, 163
  real estate, 185, 190, 195, 197
  investing, 174, 212
  mentor, 229
postdiction, 193
Power Tips Unscripted, 241
preconstruction work, 7, 19, 39, 75, 78, 85-87, 109, 115, 165
prediction, 158, 193
present day value (PV), 151-153, 181, 232
price-to-earnings ratios (PE), 220
principles, iv, 8, 12, 26, 113, 114, 133-139, 167, 229
pro bono, 226
procedures, 12, 18-23, 56, 82, 100, 104, 105, 107, 177, 227, 240
production manager (PM), 36, 48, 92
productivity, 18, 87, 92, 93, 115, 232, 246
profit
  banks, 102
  bidding, 97
  branding, 81
  calculating profit, 95
  capital gain, 244
  cash reserves, 68, 72
  consultants, 51
  contracts, 75
  debt, 176
  dividend, 245
  falling profits, 81
  house flipping, 186, 201, 208

profit *(Continued)*
　increasing profits, 83-85, 98, 99
　investing, 50
　leads, 103, 132
　margins, 48, 61, 100, 133, 175
　marketing, 77
　overhead, 48, 49, 127
　owner's pay, 55, 57, 101, 124
　planning, 58, 59
　pro bono, 94
　profit and loss statement (P&L), 104, 105, 247
　profit costs, 70-72, 81, 101, 116, 117, 126, 176, 179, 233, 236, 248
　profit percentages, 17
　profit sharing, 120, 182
　profit-comes-first theory, 32
　project selection, 54, 56, 79
　protecting profit, 107, 109, 114, 118
　quality work, 82, 165
　responsibility, 44, 126
　selling price, 181
　sharing, 174
　stocks and bonds, 215
　undercharge, 69, 70, 73
　wages, 65, 249
project manager, 37, 67-69, 84, 85, 99, 115, 184
property operation, 202
prospects, search for, 198
purchasing power, 135, 136, 166, 192, 247
purpose, iv, vii, 12, 13, 53, 55-61, 90, 99, 102, 152, 167, 174, 200, 229
purposeful thinking, 56
PV. *See* present day value

quality
　materials, 31
　relationships, 56
　distractions, 60
　estimates, 86, 100
　value, 203, 249
　quality control, 22, 32, 80-83, 107, 165
　workmanship, 17, 23, 35, 49, 189
quotes
　verbal, 90

quotes *(Continued)*
　written, 19, 86, 87, 90, 91, 93

RainCatcher, 178
rainy days, 126
Rajan, Deva, 175, 239, 252
Ramsey, David, 240
real dollars, 146, 164, 247, 248
real estate
　cash, 136
　construction pro advantages, 186-195, 209
　diversify, 136, 213
　down markets, 140, 152
　fluctuations, 157
　frictional costs, 161
　Graham and Bogle, 130
　investing, 185-209, 239, 244
　managers, 209
　margin of safety, 135
　ownership, 214
　purchasing land, 185
　rentals, 222
　S&P 500, 132
　taxes, 125, 168, 169, 186
　valuations, 150-155
realized profits, 100
rebalance, 219, 248
receivables, 104, 105, 248
recession, 3, 8, 37-40, 51, 59, 68, 98, 119, 134, 147, 150, 152, 179, 189, 193, 202, 212
Reed, John, 208,
Remodelers Advantage, 127, 241
Remodeling Life, The, 174
rent
　contract, 112, 190, 203-205
　insurance, 112, 202, 205
　property, 133, 152, 154, 188, 190, 194, 198, 202-209
　protections, 112
reputation, 4, 17, 32, 33, 128, 176, 198
resources. *See* Essential Resources, 239-241
respect, 23, 36-43, 76, 80, 115, 173, 205, 249
retirement, 9, 29, 68, 145, 146, 163

retroactive clairvoyance, 193
risk
  consultants, 51
  insurance, 111
  justification, 70
  lowering risk, 144
  risk aversion, 23
  risk management, 24, 25, 133, 153, 179
  risk-free (almost) investments, 153, 154, 157
  speculation, 143
  work volume, 98, 101, 179, 180, 183
robo-managers, 98, 159, 162
Rosenthal, Michael, 251
Rosenthal, Pam, 251
Ruiz, Fernando Pagés, 81, 239, 241, 252
Running a Successful Construction Company, 240

S&P 500, 131, 132, 155, 158, 159, 248
safe workplace, 40
salary, 36, 65, 149, 245, 247, 248. *See also* draw
sales
  calls, 22, 48, 78, 175
  value, 180
  volume, 17, 134
Schleifer, Thomas, 117, 239
Schwarz, Charles, 30, 33
security, 174, 178, 248, 249
self-defeating ideas, 45
selling (your company), 176-183
selling price, 181, 182, 249
selling, general, and administrative expenses (SGA), 47, 48, 50
selling, social, 79
SGA (see selling, general, and administrative expenses)
Shiller, Robert, 150, 192, 220, 221, 231
short-term cost, 42
site inspection, 22, 93, 233
site inspection checklist, 233
skills trades, 90, 222
Small Giants, 41, 42, 82, 180, 240
snowball, 164, 240
socially responsible fund, 248

speculation, 139-143, 150, 151, 194
speculative bubble, 149, 150
spreadsheet, 93, 115, 249
Stanley, Tom, 27, 28, 240
Staples, Wally, 173, 174, 178, 208, 211, 241
stockbroker, 162, 183, 214-218, 246
stocks, investing
  brokers, 214, 215
  cash, 136
  companies, 212, 213
  frictional costs, 162, 167
  margin of safety, 135
  market performance, 214, 215, 246
  market price, 152
  present value, 154, 155
  speculation, 141
  taxes, 168
  temperament, 147, 150
  time, 145
  See alpha investors
  See exchange traded funds (ETFs)
  See index funds
  See mutual funds
Stoddard, Joe, 84, 85
subcontractor, 2, 5, 6, 244, 249. *See also* trade partners
supplier quotes, 19, 87, 90, 93
survivor bias, 195
Sutton, Garrett, 240
sweet spot, 79, 80
system building, 24
systematic procedures, 21
systems, business
  education, 6, 25, 26, 222
  estimates, 22
  lean systems, 117, 164
  marketing program, 18
  owner-centered, 177
  procedures, 20, 21
  profit, 73
  purposeful thinking, 56
  "Resources," 239
  testing, 175
  using systems, 21

tax audit, 236

taxes
  liabilities, 52
  employment, 84
  evasion, 124, 125, 178
  cash, 128, 155
  rate of gain, 148
  costs, 153, 167, 169, 170
  retirement account, 163
  inflation, 166
  tax brackets, 168
  construction pro advantage, 186
teachers, 16, 222. *See also* mentors
technology, 54, 134, 135, 212
tenants, 166, 187-191, 194, 202-208, 211, 212, 217
termination (firing), 21, 108
theft, 71, 236
thinking errors, 45-47, 146, 168
Thomas, Jason, 178
thought remodeling (see cognitive behavioral therapy)
time efficiency, 29, 84, 85, 165
time value of money, 52, 56, 84, 132, 135, 157, 191, 203, 246, 248, 249
Tim Faller Show, The, 11, 241
title company, 161
TMF (see traditional mutual fund)
tools, viii, 17, 19, 43, 44, 48, 50, 52, 66, 67, 91, 104, 151, 164, 173, 231, 235, 237
Total Money Makeover, 240
Traction, 22, 53, 180
trade partners (subcontractors)
  bids, 71, 90, 91, 115
  quality, 17, 31
  respect, 23, 37, 42, 43, 79, 115
  production builders, 25
  stinginess, 32
  direct costs, 47, 65, 70, 244
  overhead, 48, 96, 97
  designers, 71
  estimates, 87, 90, 92
  numbers, 89

trade partners *(Continued)*
  included/not included form, 93, 233
  skills, 94
  relationships, 104, 165, 249
  communication, 113, 114
  payment, 125, 127, 247
tradesman, 5, 22
traditional mutual fund (TMF), 215, 216, 218
Tremper, Deb, 252
typical progression, 17

Uhler, Bryan, 65
Uhler, Tim, 65
underbidding, 70, 112, 127, 133
undercharging, 133
underestimator, 93
underpricing, 45, 236
underthinking, 53, 56
underwater, 143, 193

vacancy factor, 142, 153, 199
value engineering, 165, 249
vandalism, 236
Vanguard, 16, 129, 155, 213, 215-217, 219, 220

wages, 40, 41, 65, 84, 174, 249
Wally J. Staples Builders, Inc., 173
war chest, 126
warning bells, 109
waste, 30, 31, 44, 84, 90, 107, 124, 192, 222
weather, 70, 92, 119
website, ESOPS, 241
wholesale prices, 185, 201, 206
Wickman, Gino, 22, 53, 56, 60, 180
Winans, Nina, 174, 175, 177-179
Winans, Paul, 174, 175, 178
Woods, Cathie, 158, 159
work schedule, 21, 31, 39, 57, 244

YouTube, 130, 141, 227

Made in the USA
Middletown, DE
24 July 2022